PJSmith

Miracles, Magic, and Mayhem, the IMAGIKINS
First edition copyright 2013 by PJ Smith
IMAGIKINS™ is a trademark and registered
trademark of PJ Smith LLC
All rights reserved.

No part of this book may be
reproduced or utilized in whole or in part,
stored in a retrieval system, or
transmitted in any form or
by any means - electronic, mechanical,
or other - without written permission
from the publisher and copyright holder.

All inquiries, contact PJ Smith:
whirlwindpjs@gmail.com

www.IMAGIKINS.com

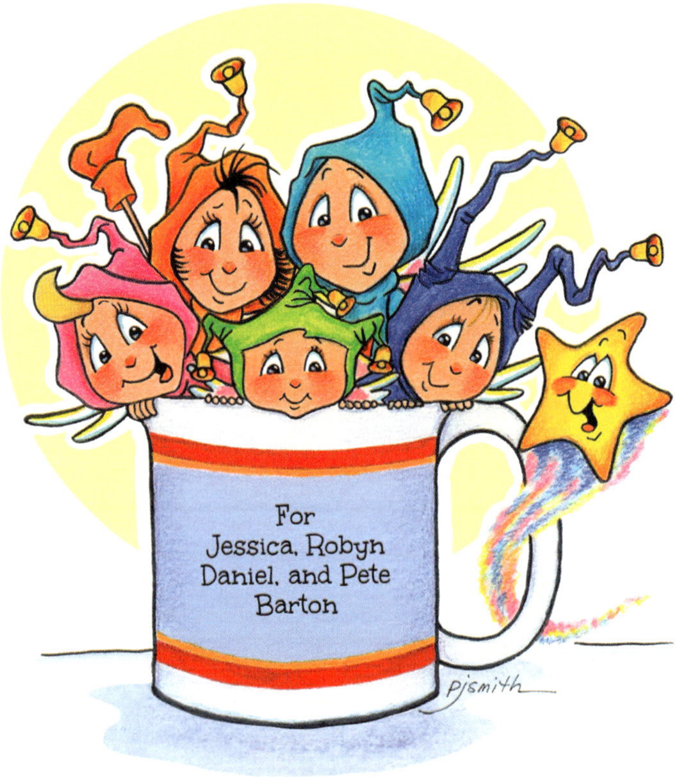
For
Jessica, Robyn
Daniel, and Pete
Barton
pjsmith

Miracles, Magic, and Mayhem

by
PJ Smith

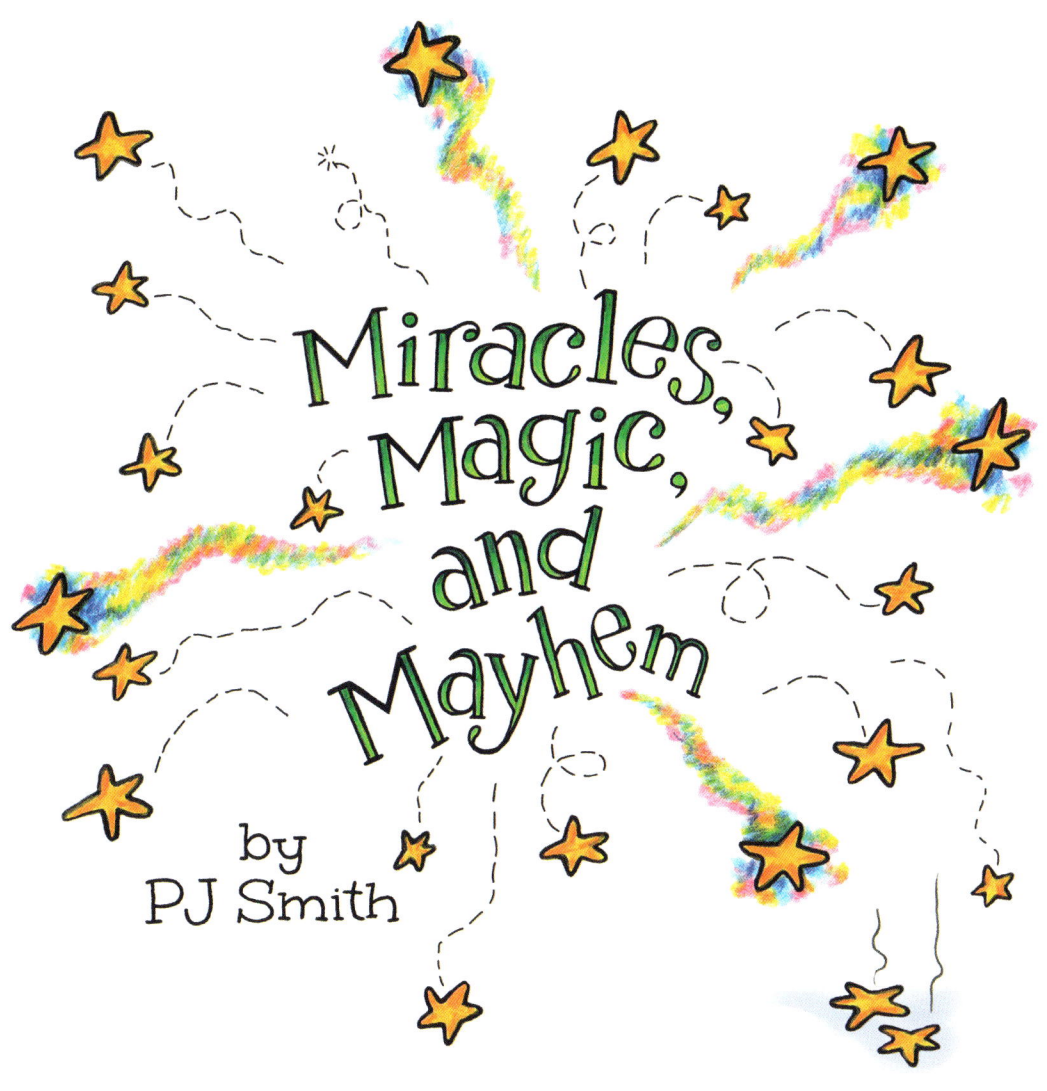

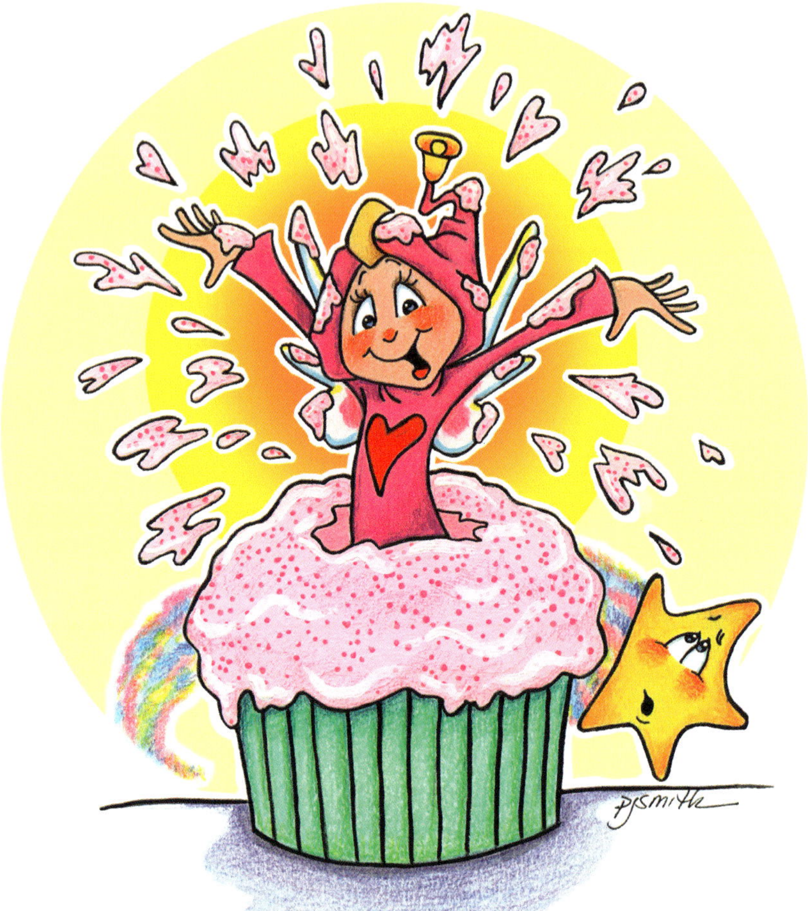
PJSMITH

Learn how to make an entrance.

A good first impression
guarantees
you will be
unforgettable.

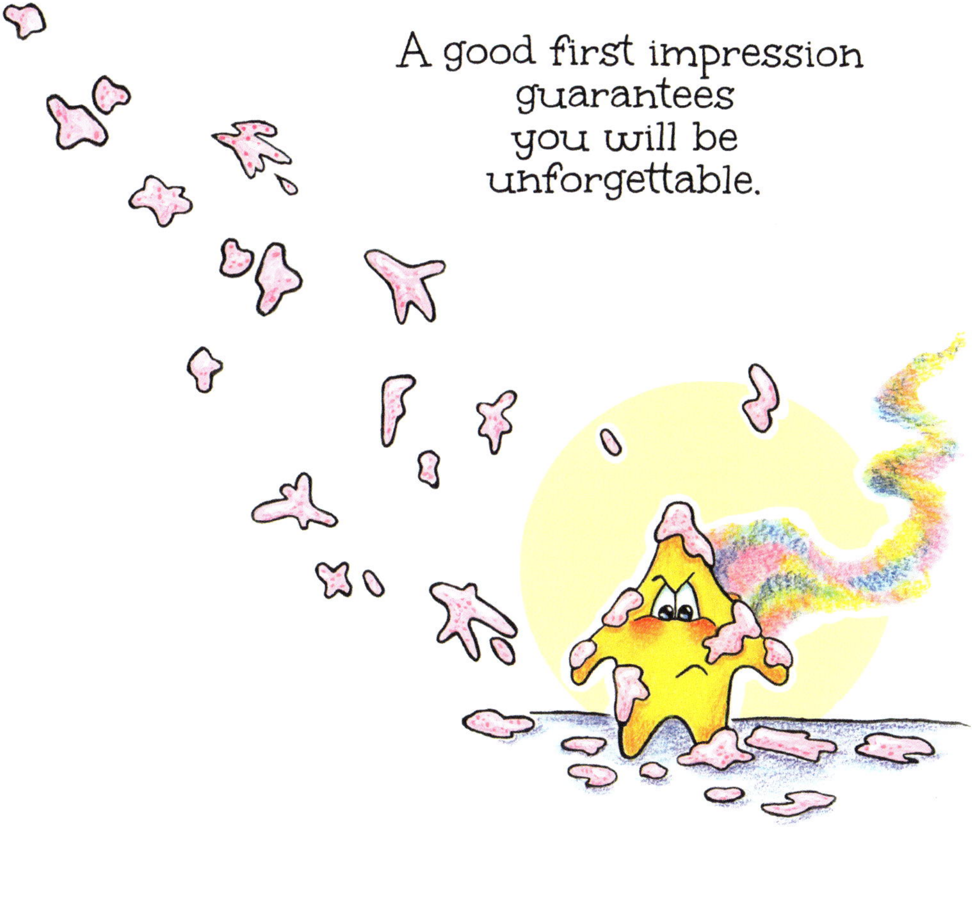

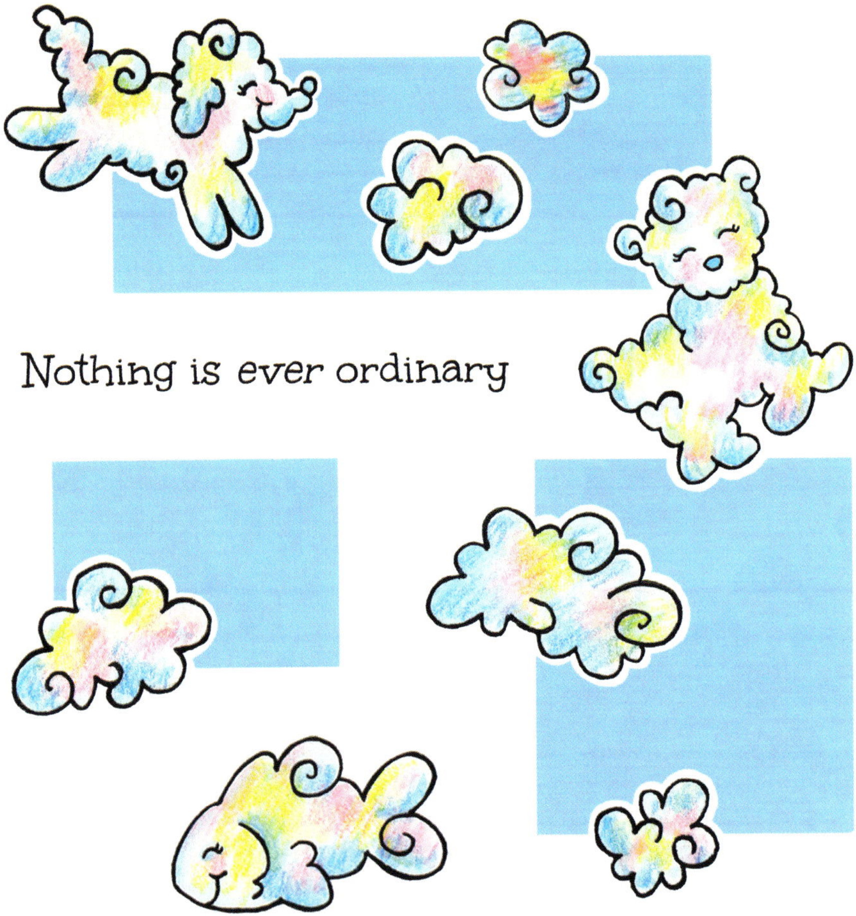

Nothing is *ever* ordinary

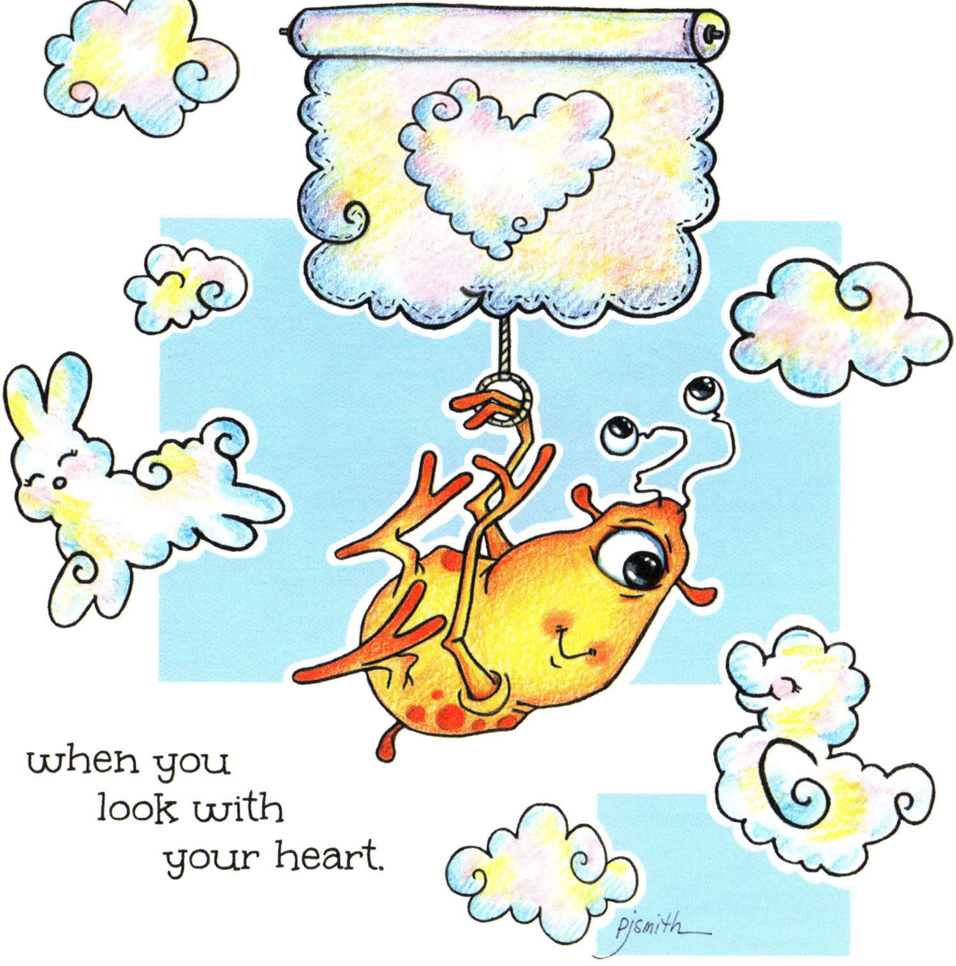
pjsmith

when you
look with
your heart.

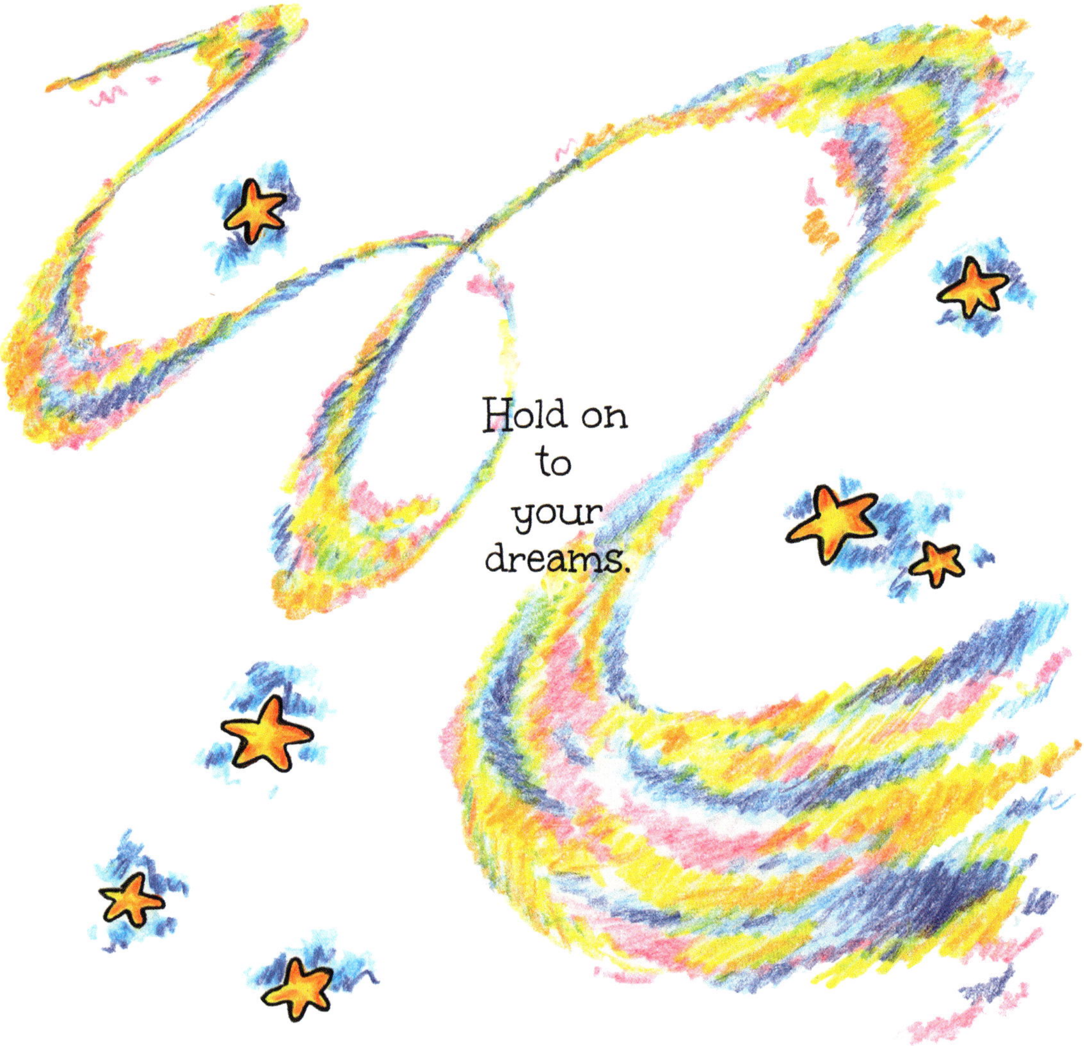

Hold on
to
your
dreams.

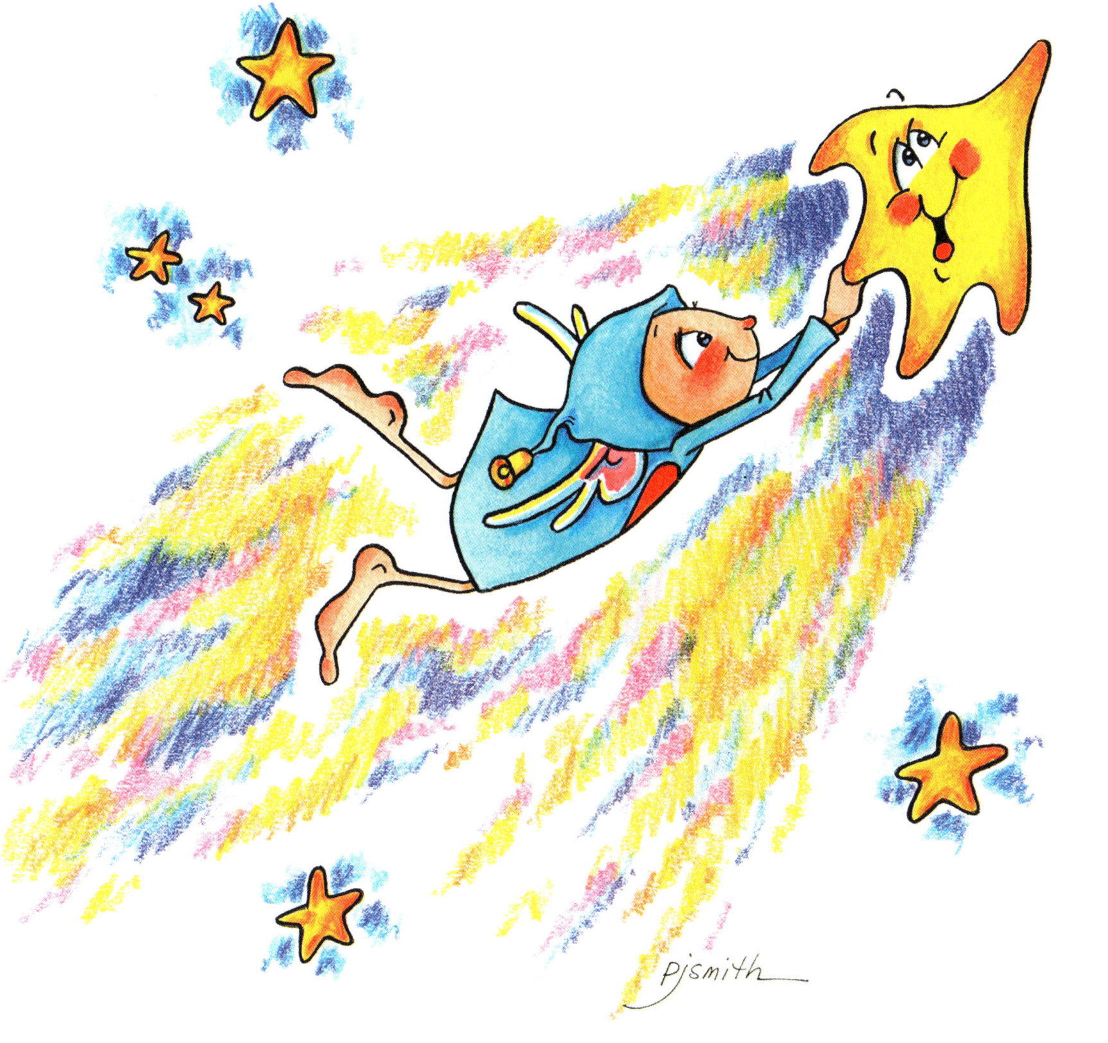
pjsmith

Adorableness
has
great power.

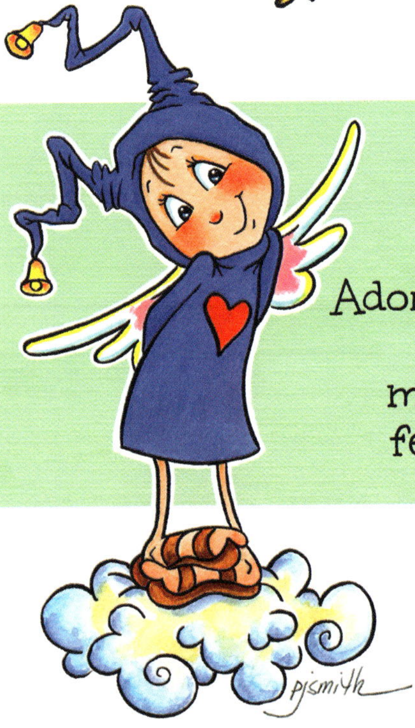
pjsmith

Adorableness
is
my best
feature.

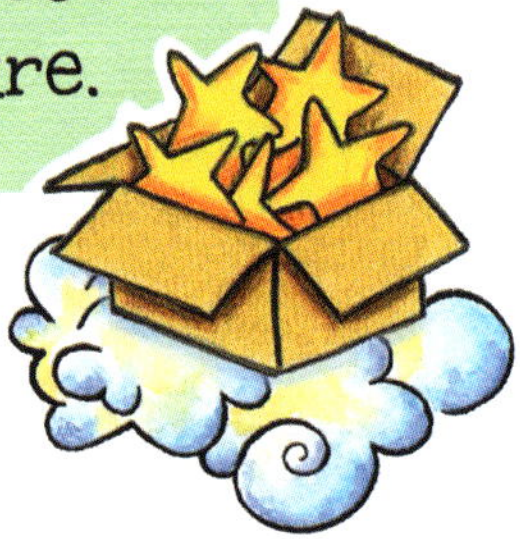

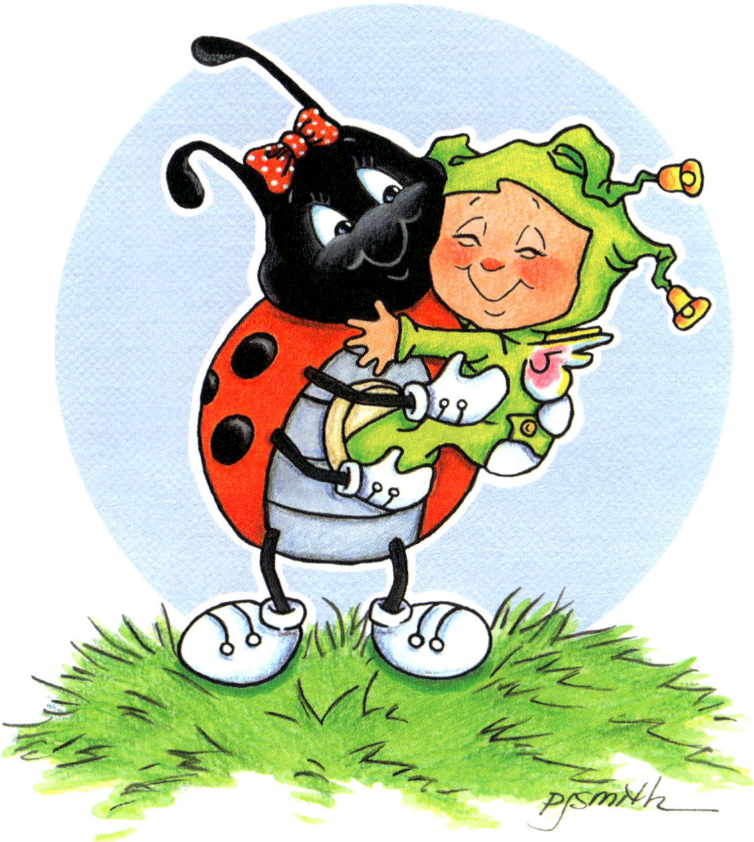
PJSmith

Bug Hugs are nice.

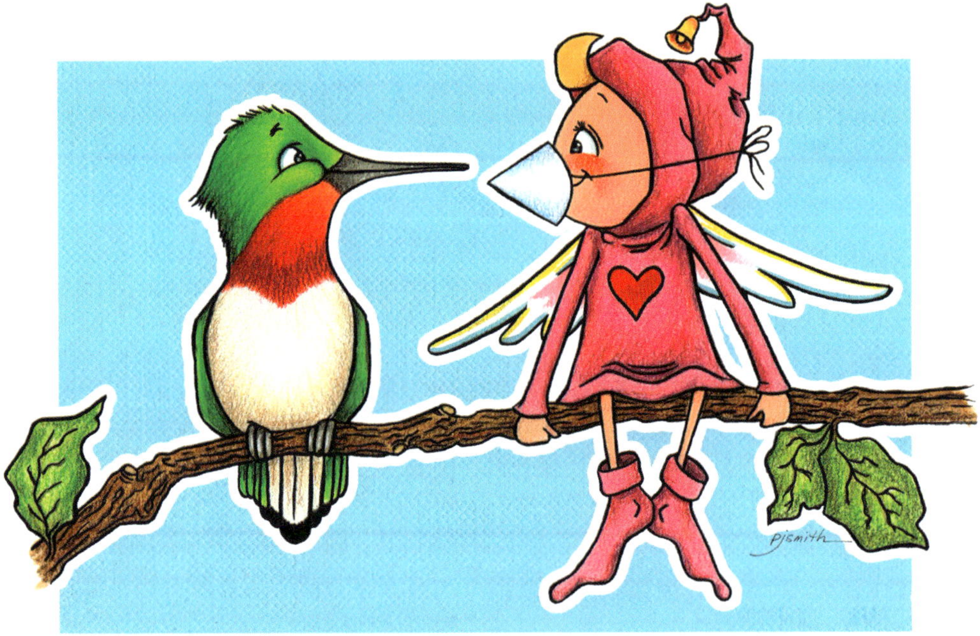
pjsmith

Birds of a feather
eventually start to look alike.

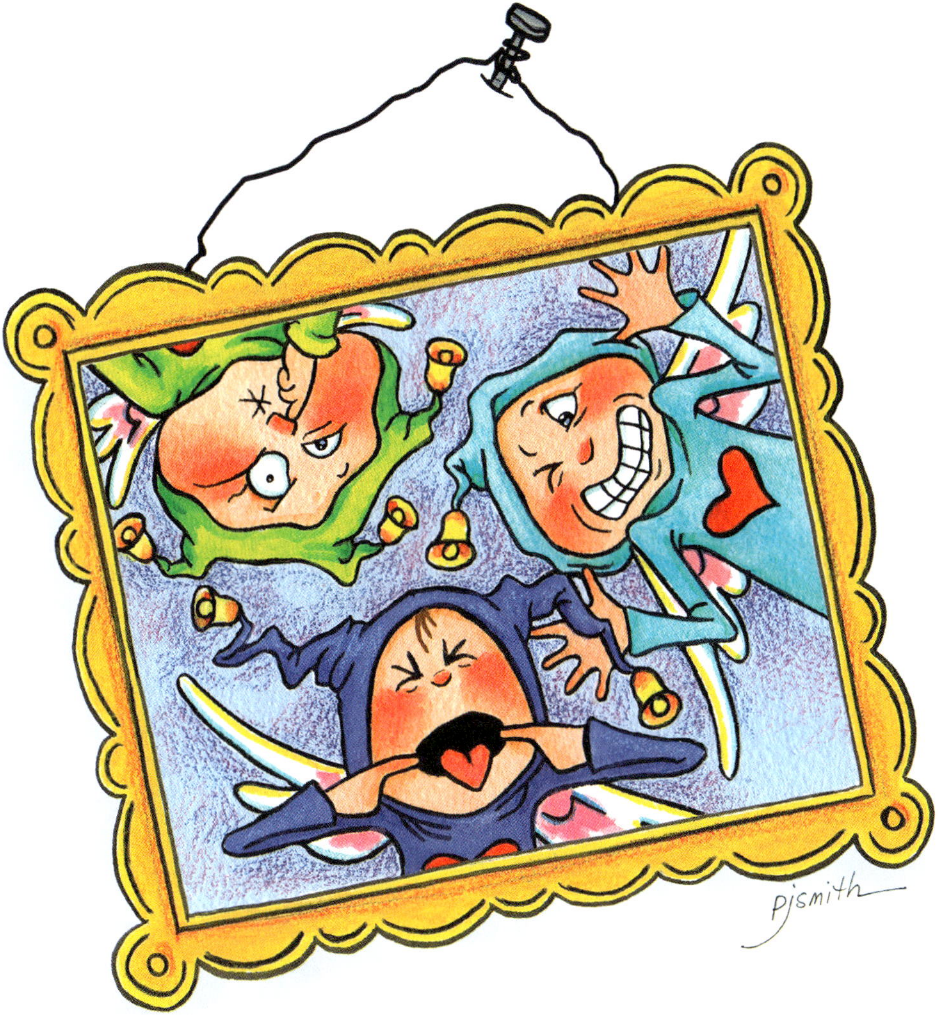
pjsmith

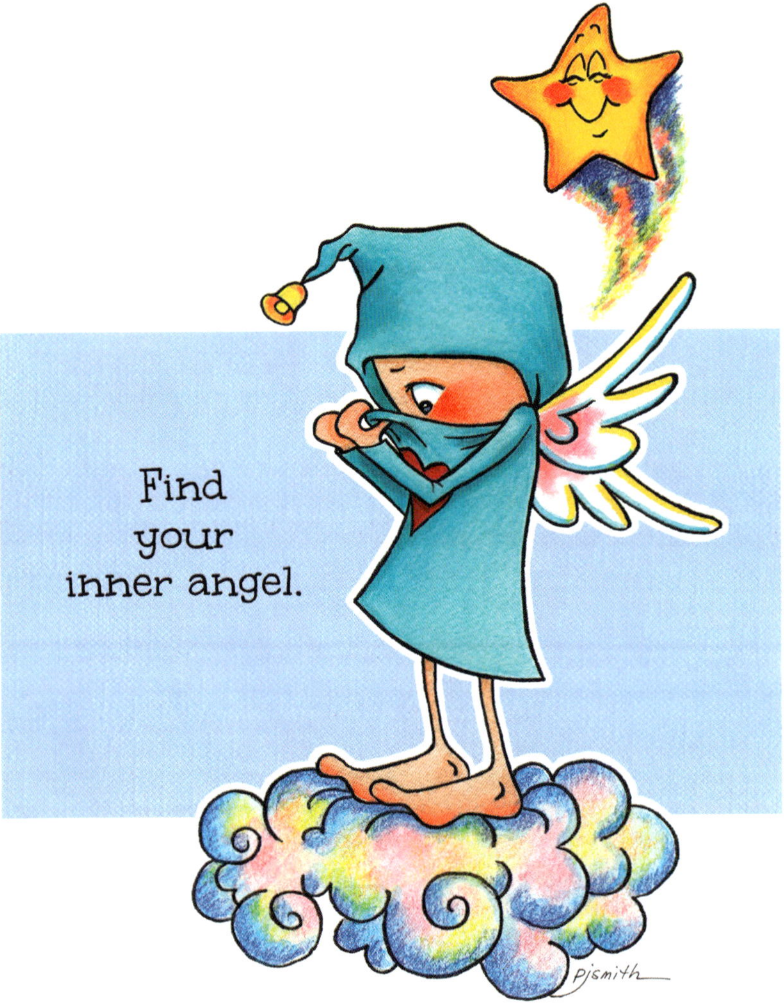
Find your inner angel.
pjsmith

Keep looking.

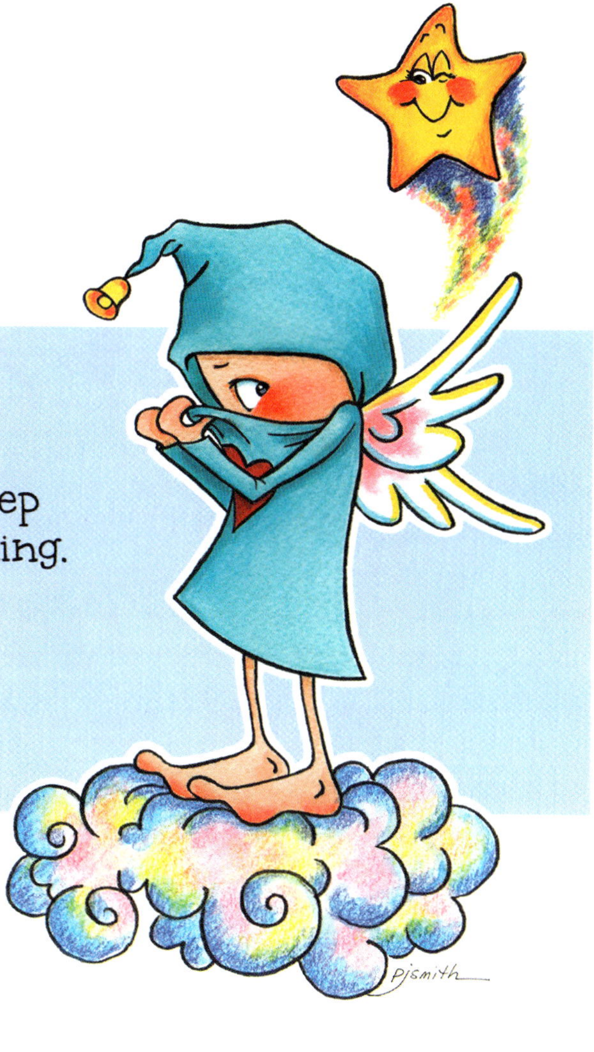
pjsmith

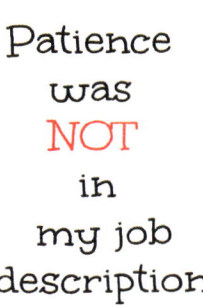
Patience was NOT in my job description.

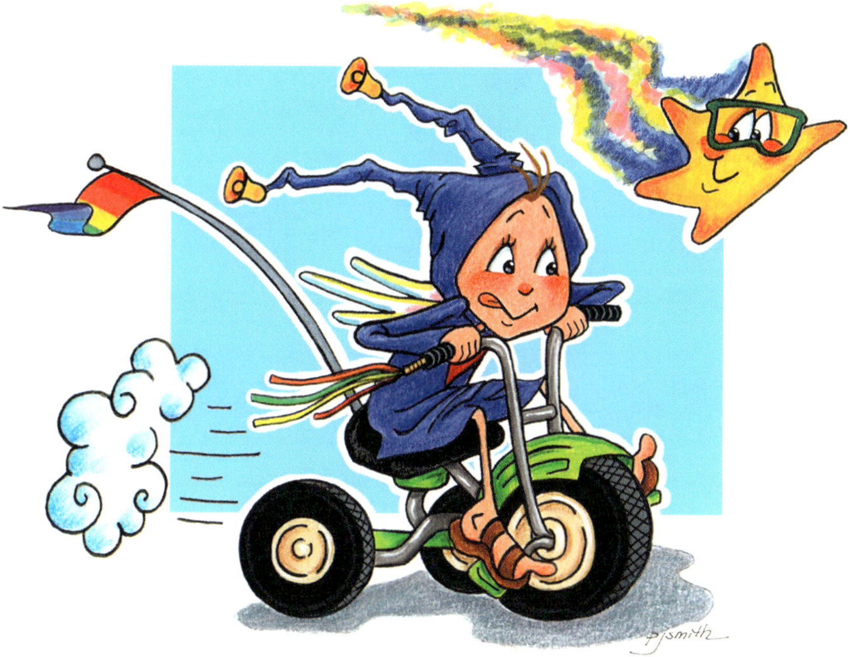
pjsmith

Born to be mild.

It's easy to blend in.
pjsmith

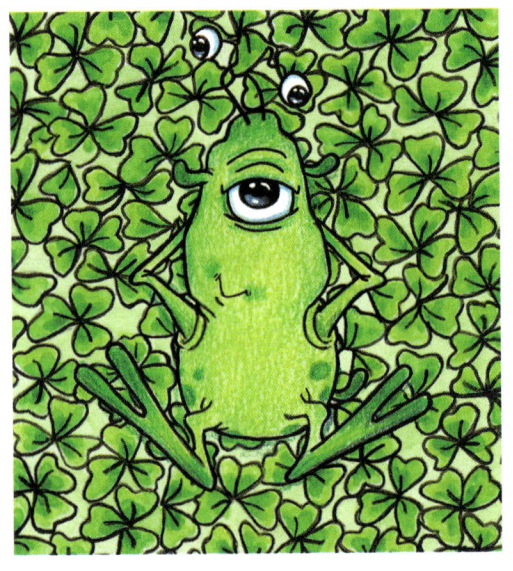

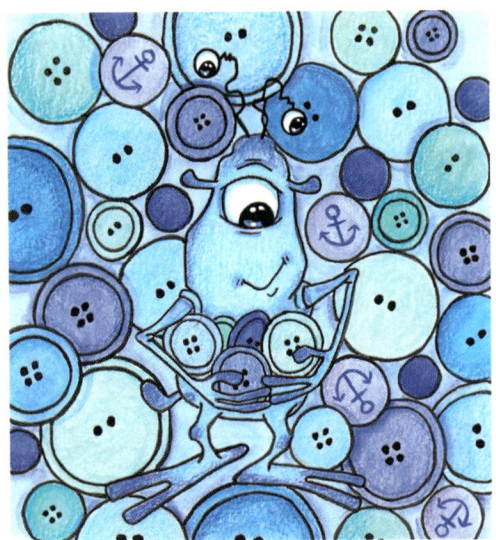

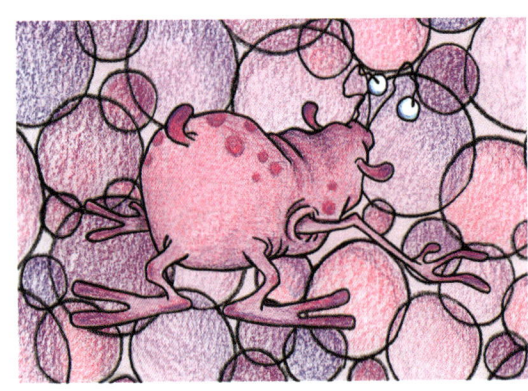

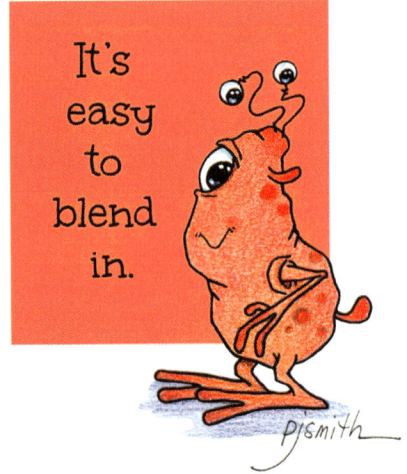

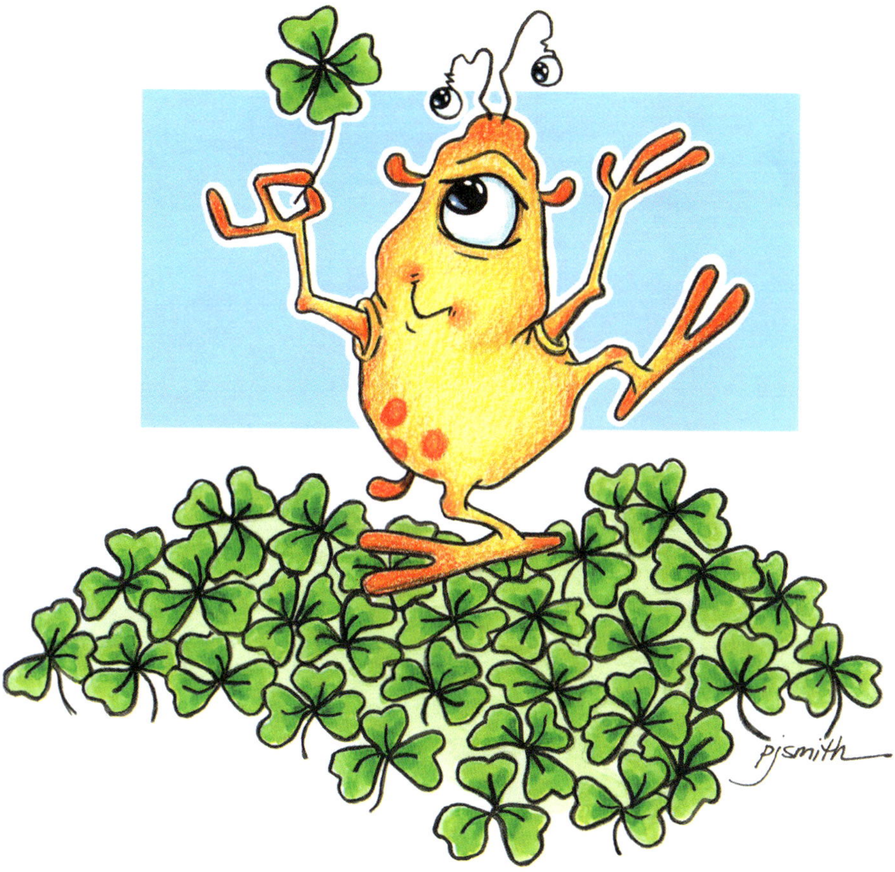
pjsmith

But you were meant to stand out.

Painting your world
with Love
is beautiful.

Painting
your friends
however,
is inadvisable.

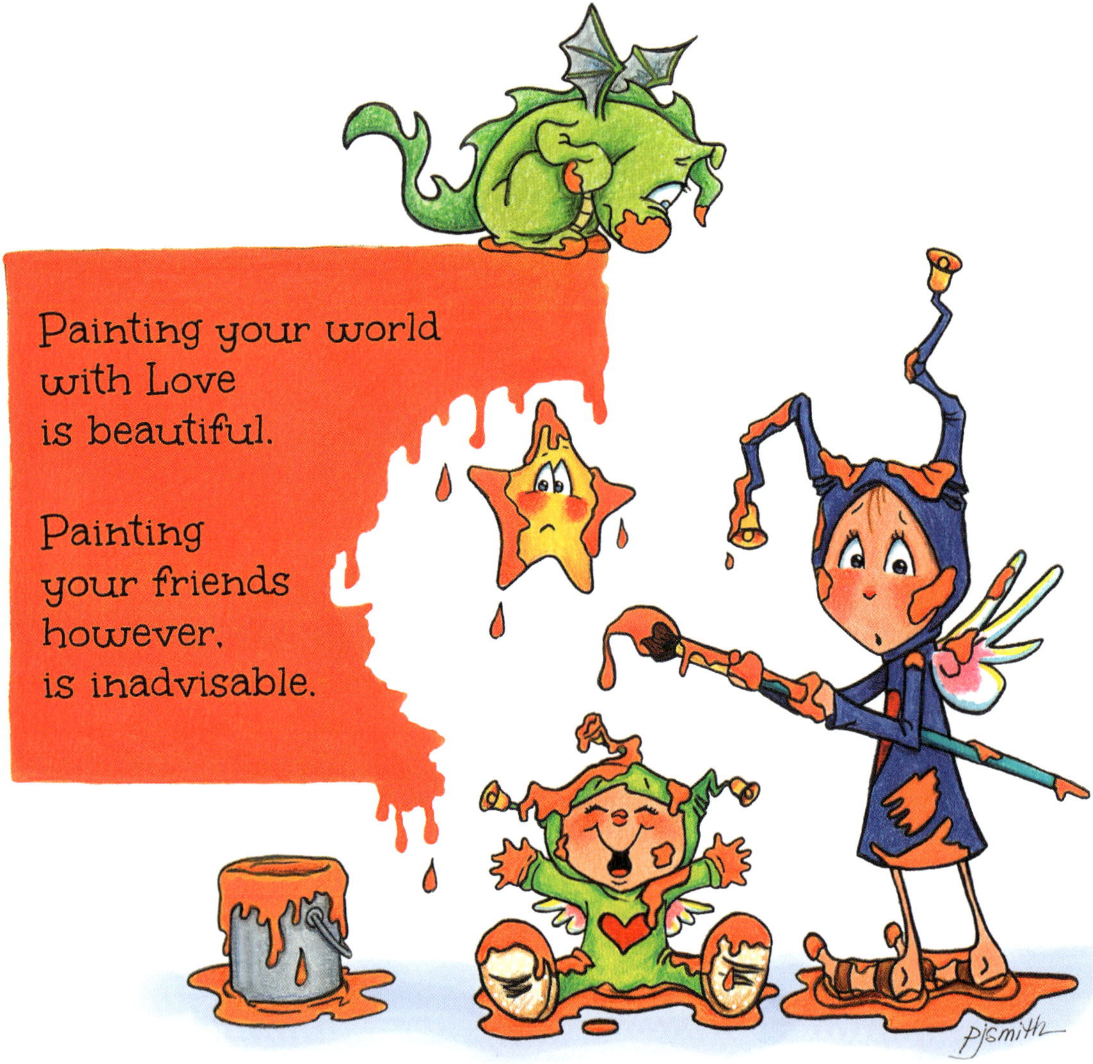
pjsmith

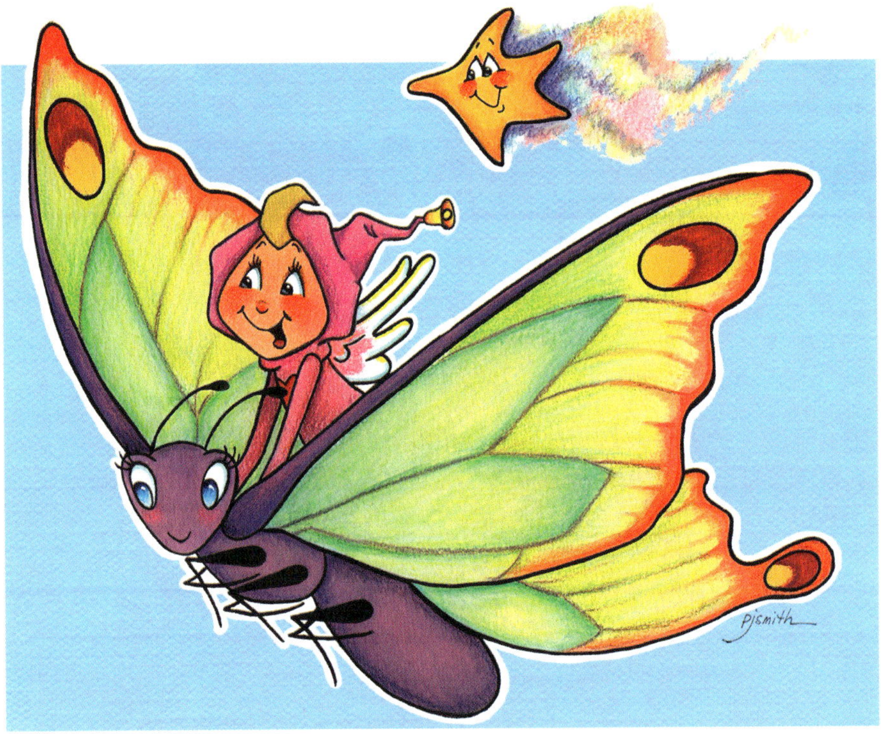
pjsmith

There are no such things
as impossible dreams.

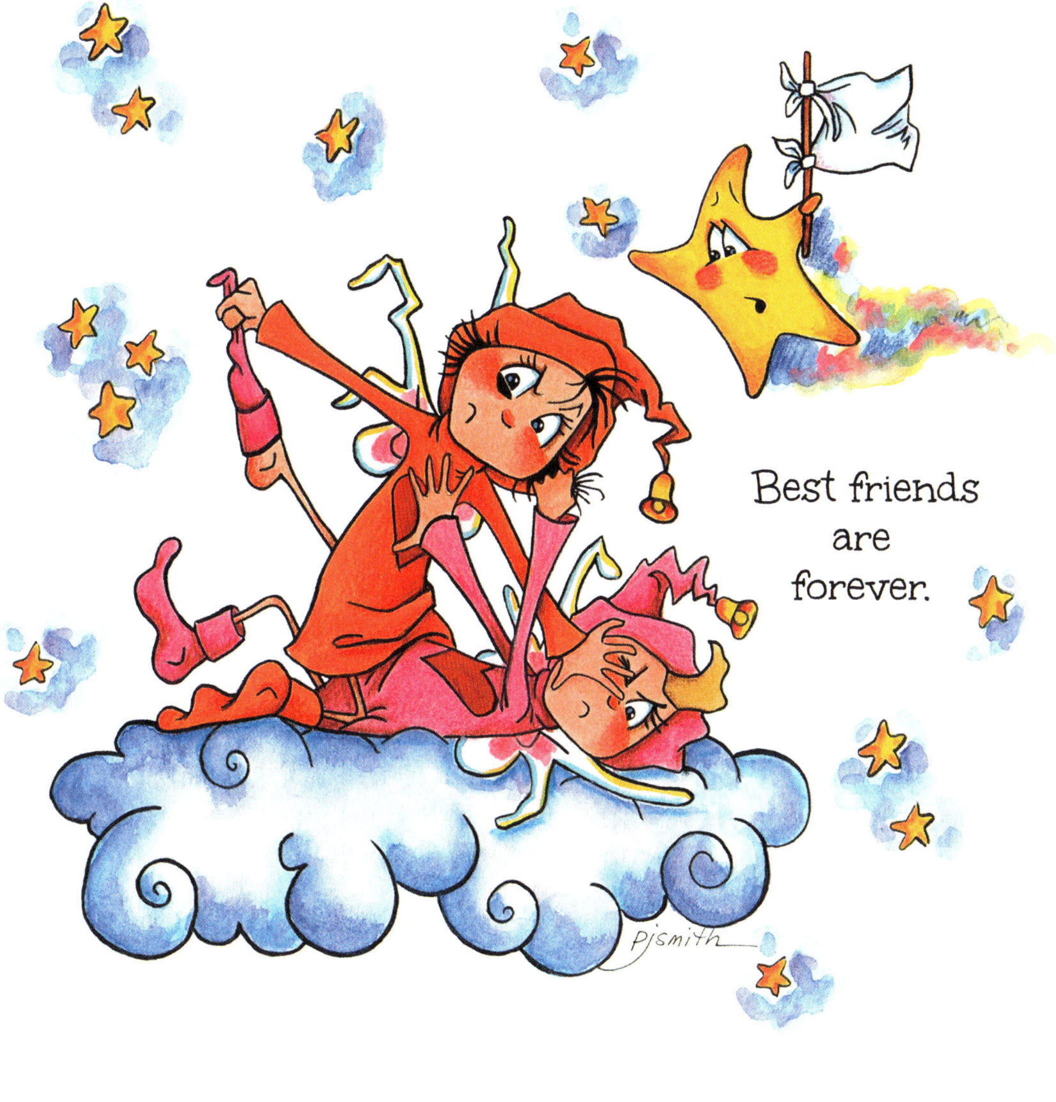
pjsmith

Best friends
are
forever.

Hurray for the up hills.
They make the down hills
more fun.

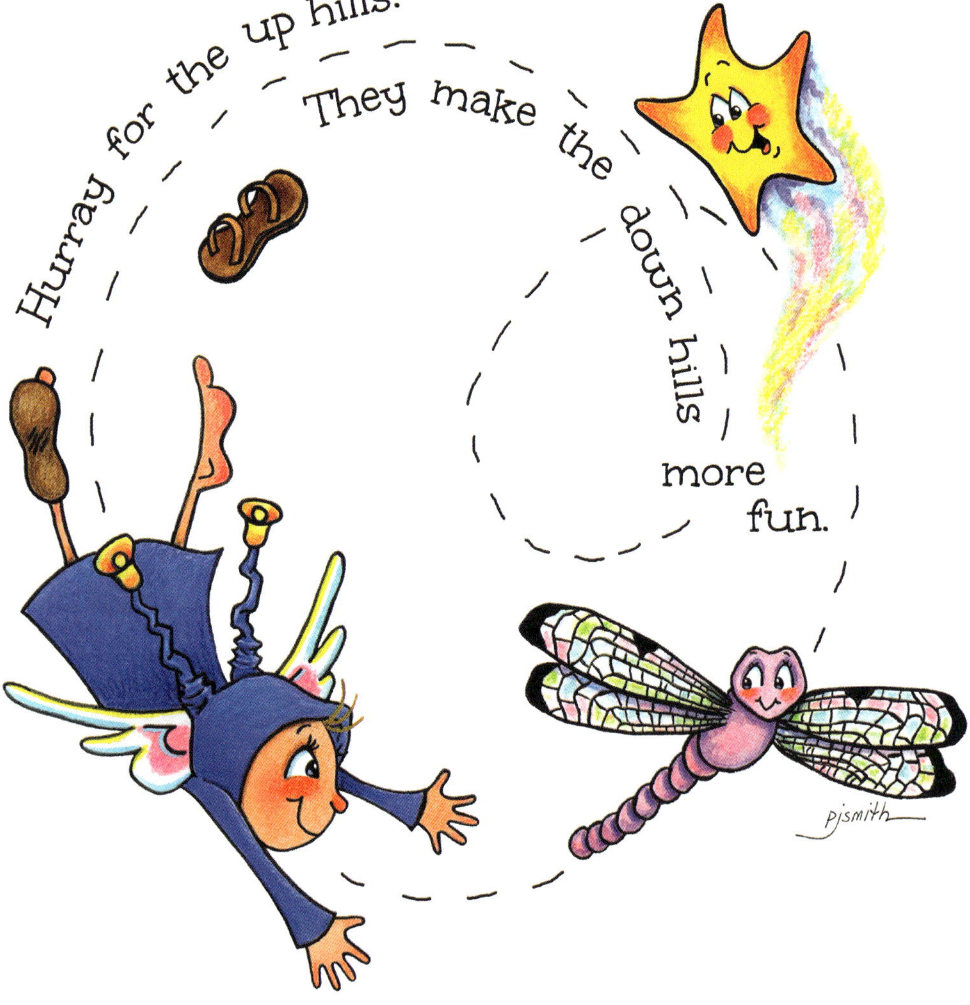
pjsmith

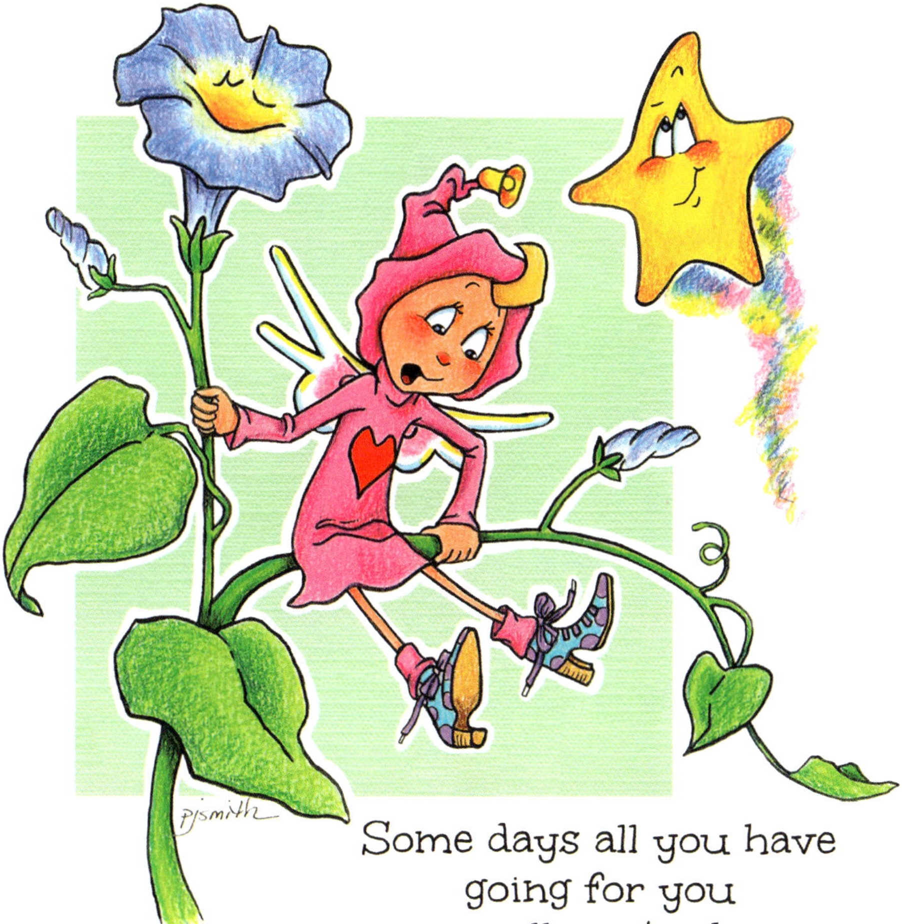
pjsmith

Some days all you have
going for you
are really cute shoes.

Dreams are guiding stars
for your heart.

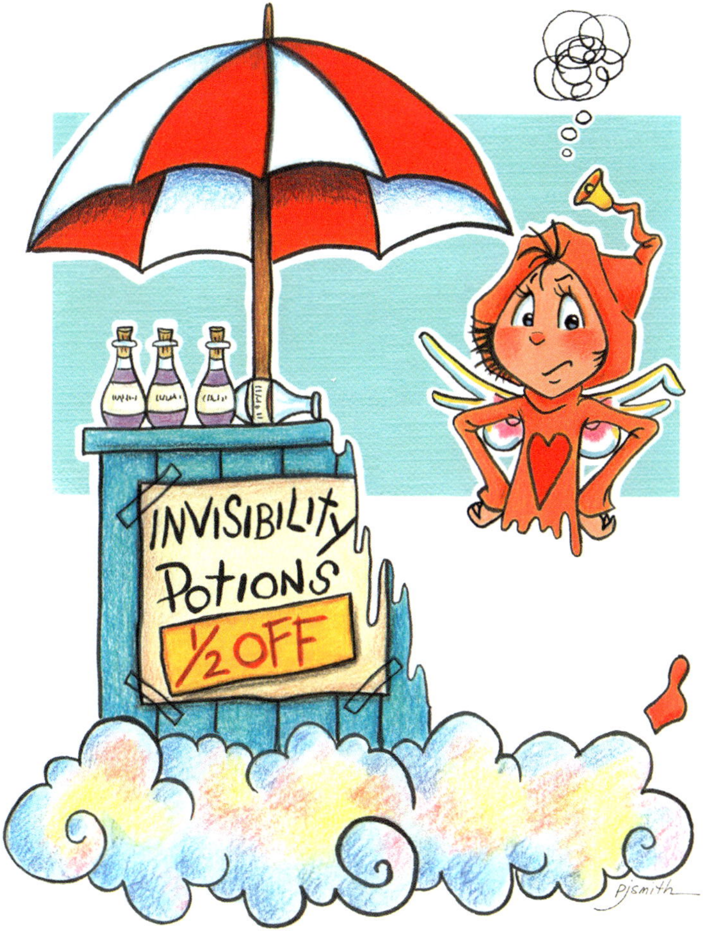
INVISIBILITY
Potions
½ OFF
pjsmith

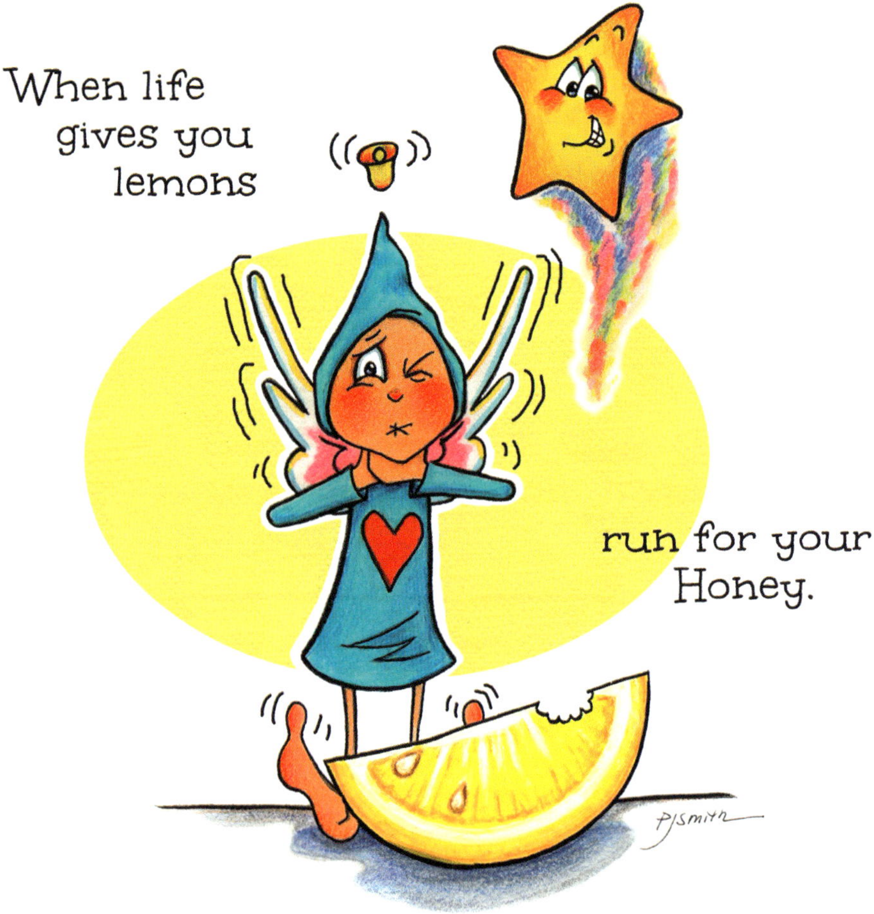
When life
gives you
lemons
run for your
Honey.

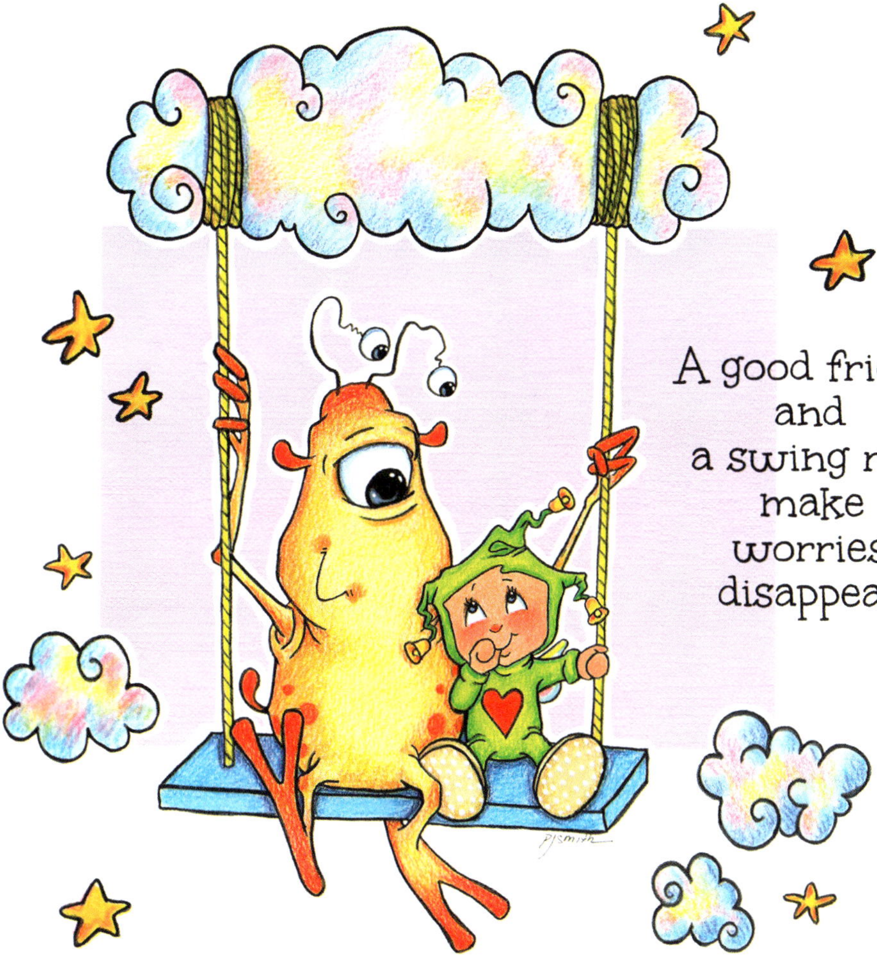

A good friend
and
a swing ride
make
worries
disappear.

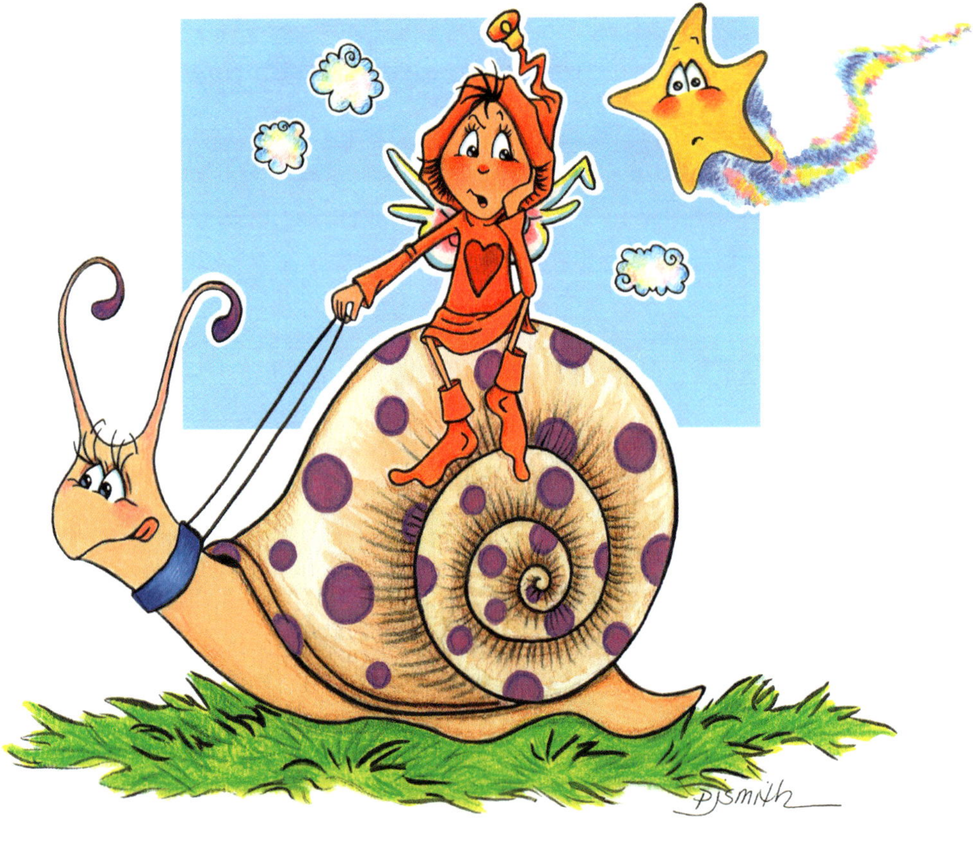
PJSmith

If I'm gonna move this slowly,
I need to learn more naughty words.

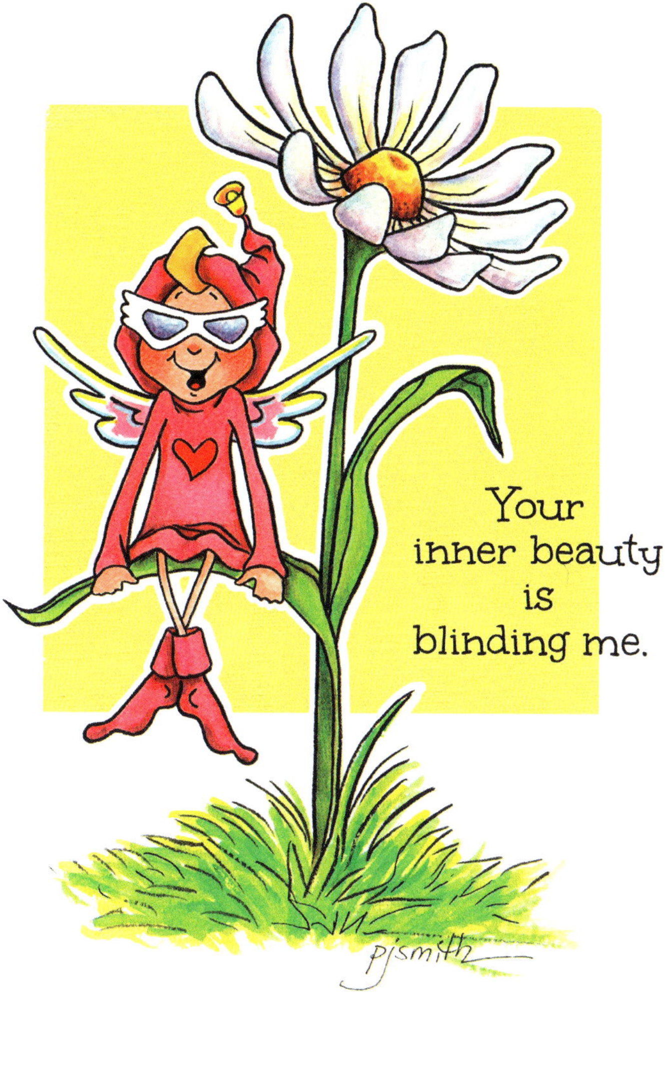
Your
inner beauty
is
blinding me.
pjsmith

I used to be normal

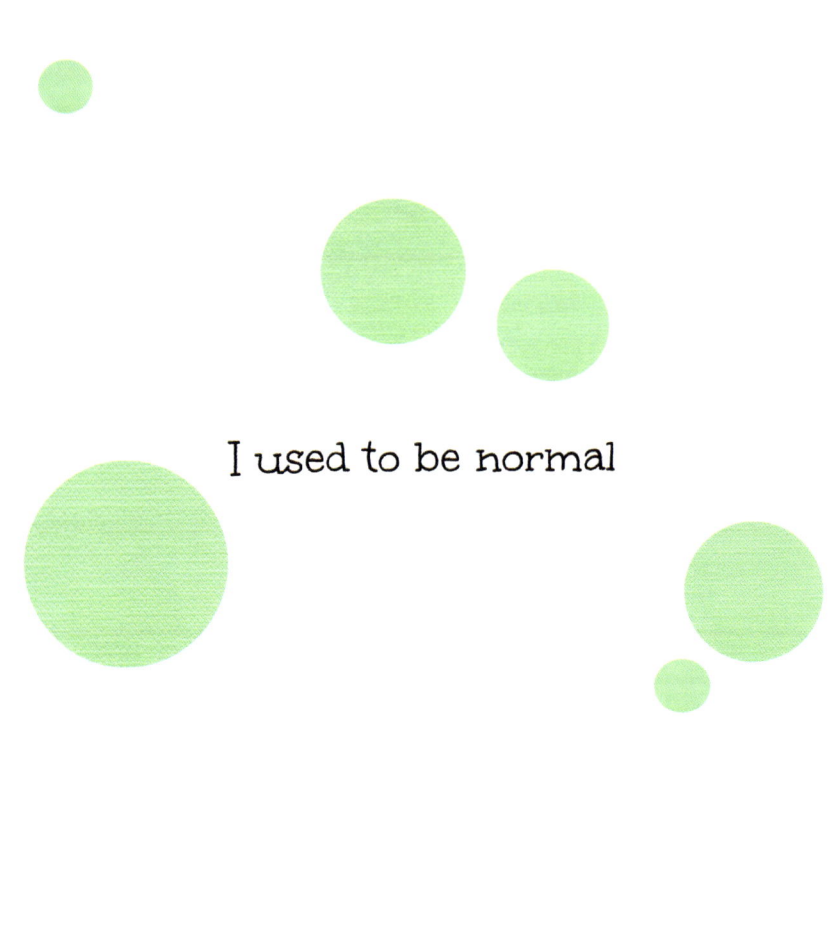

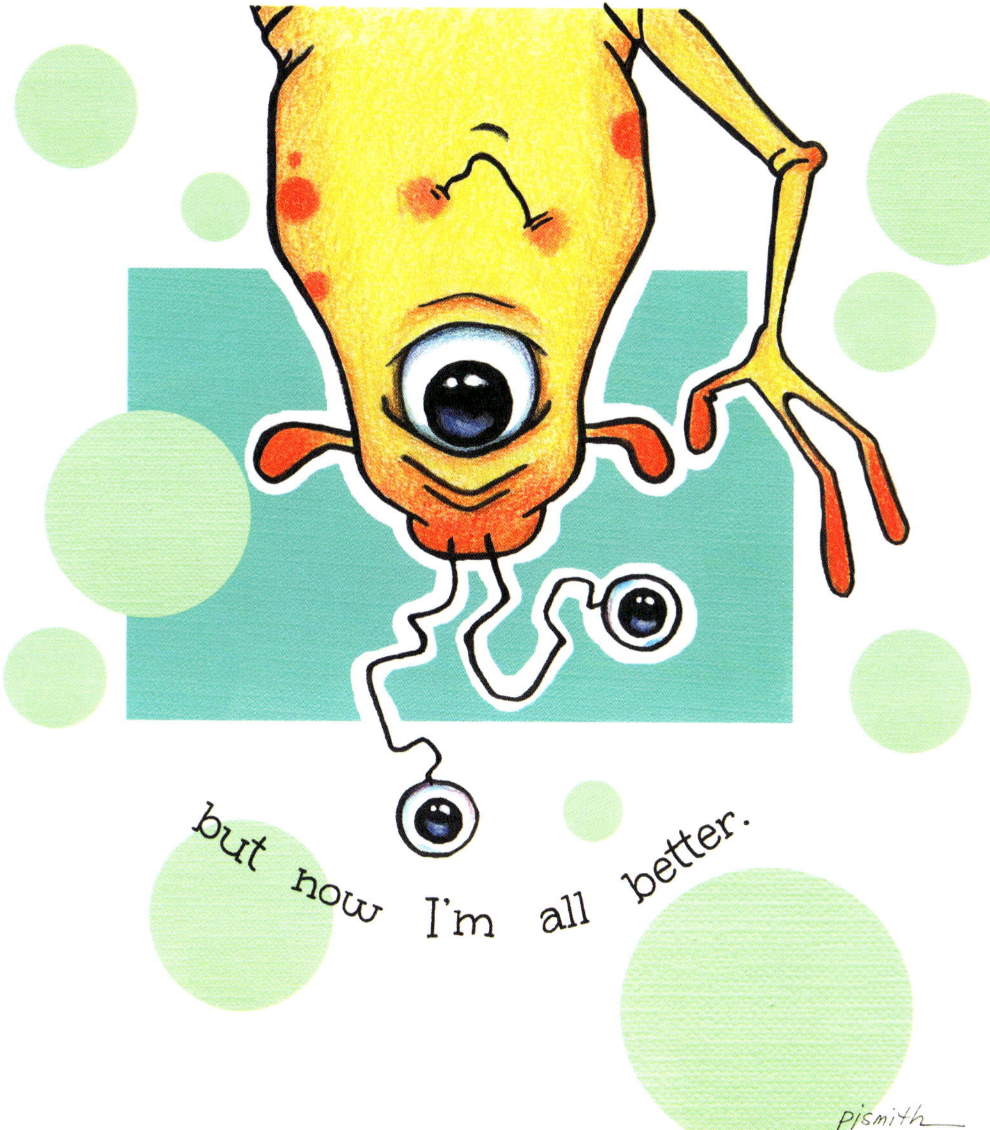
but now I'm all better.
pjsmith

You are blessed indeed.

So take the toilet paper off of your foot
and
go take on the world.

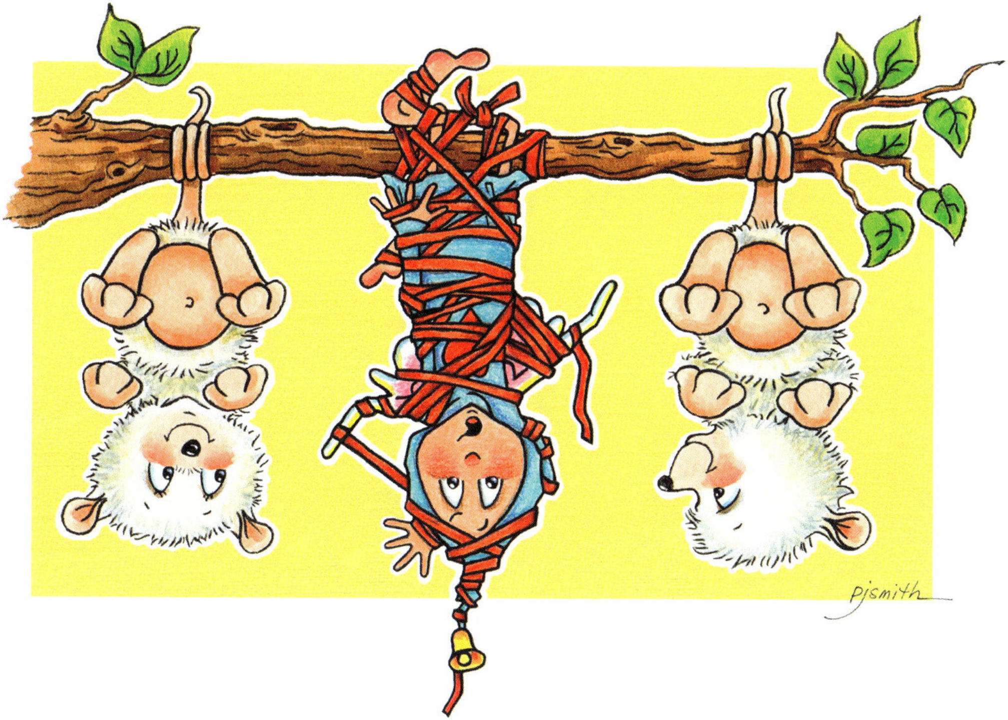
pjsmith

I've discovered that my life seems easier
if I have someone else to blame.

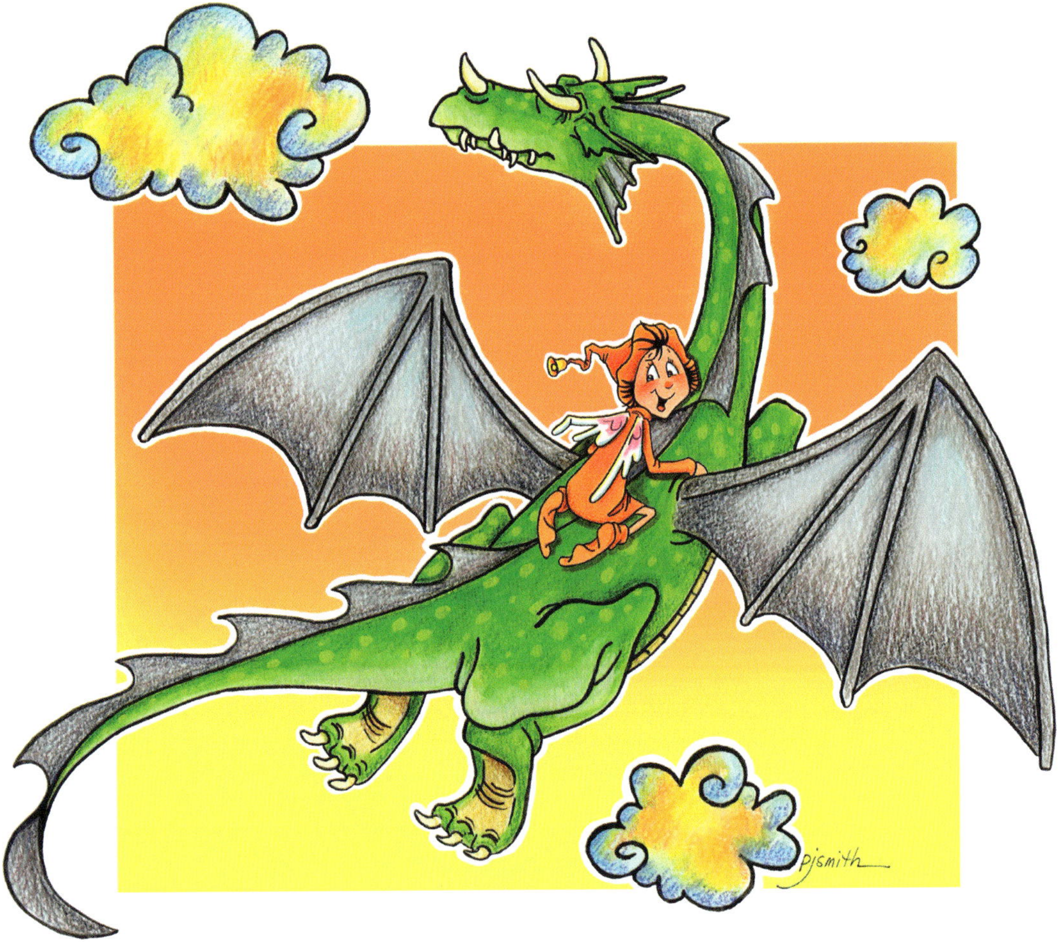
pjsmith

Being realistic
sucks all the fun out of life!

With a little Love,
a weed becomes
the flower.

pjsmith

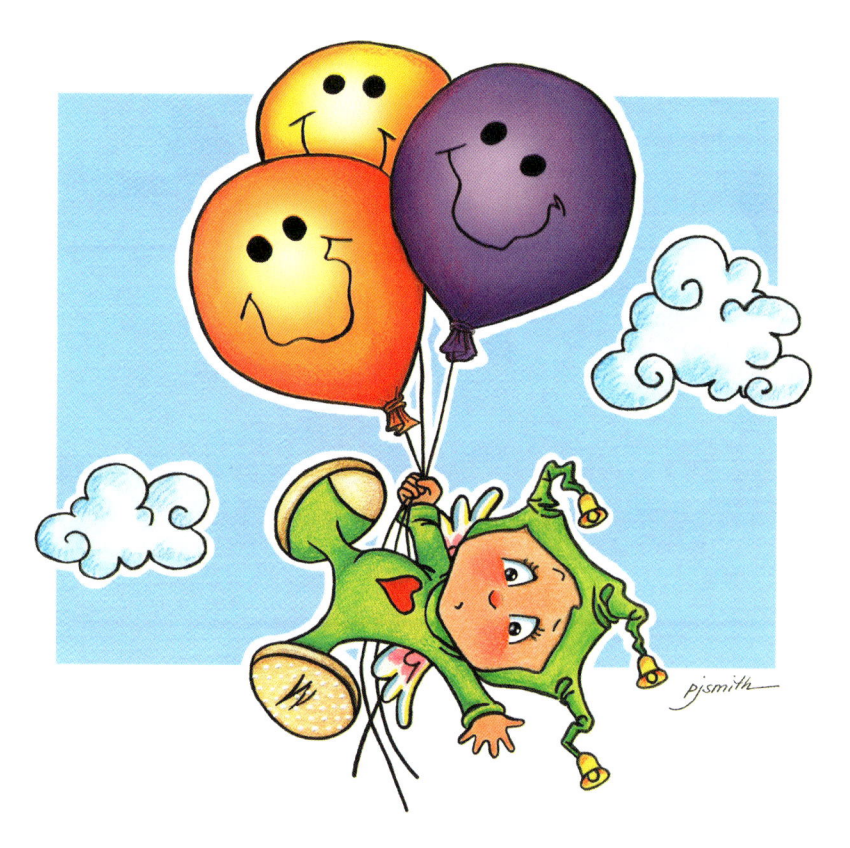

Trust your wings.

I've got them set on "vibrate".

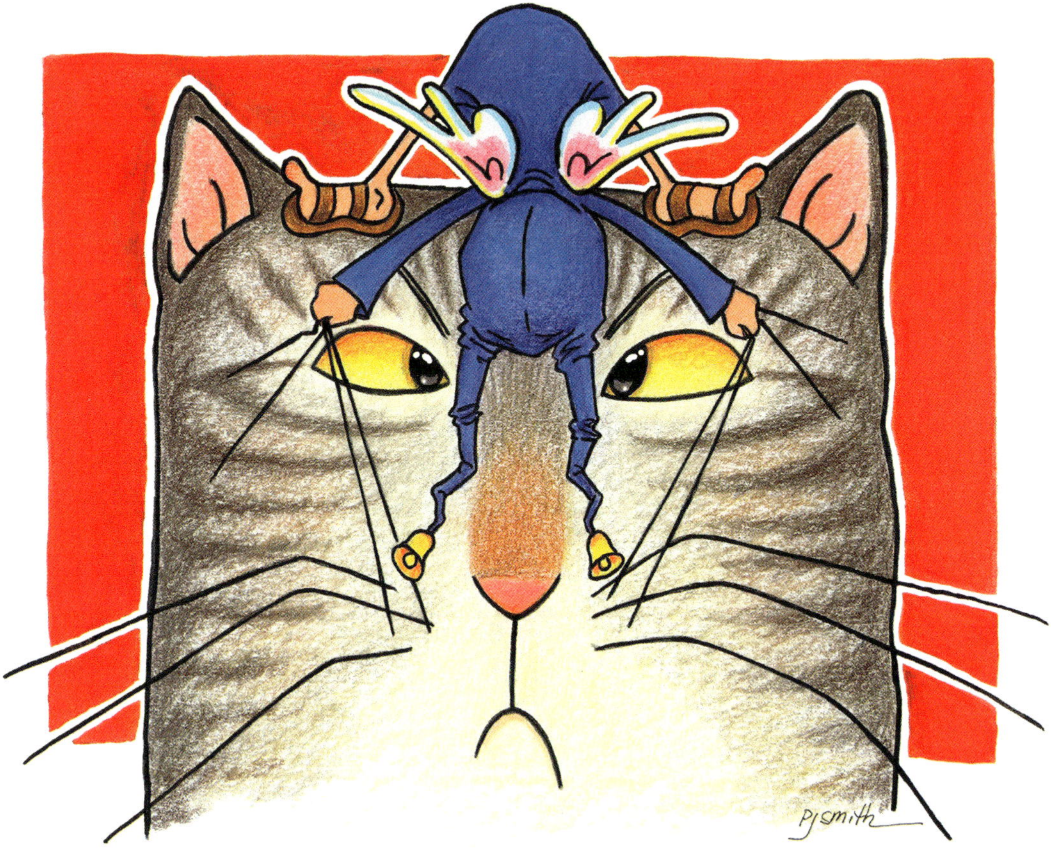
PJ Smith

When in doubt . . . DON'T.

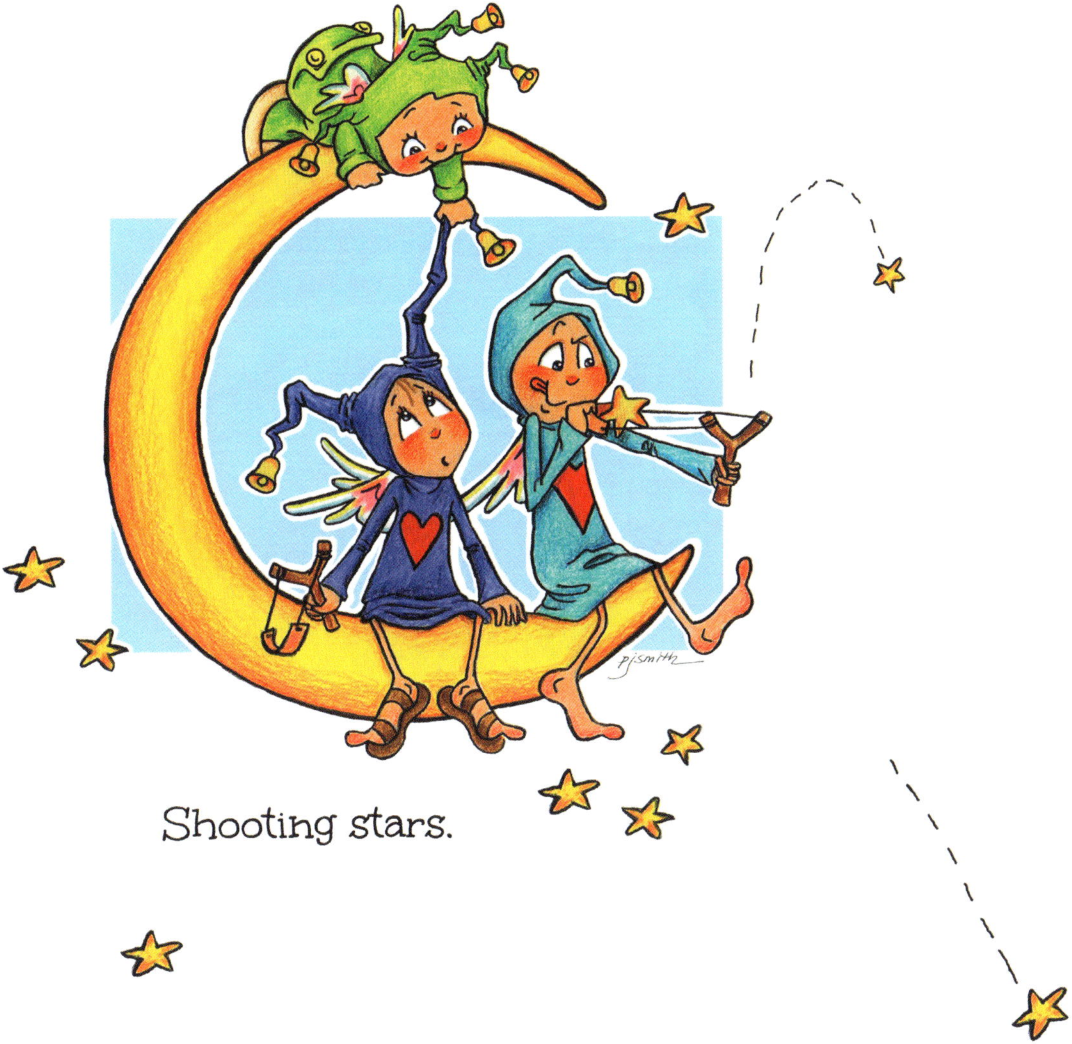

Shooting stars.

Whatever you are,
be the best "Whatever" you can be.

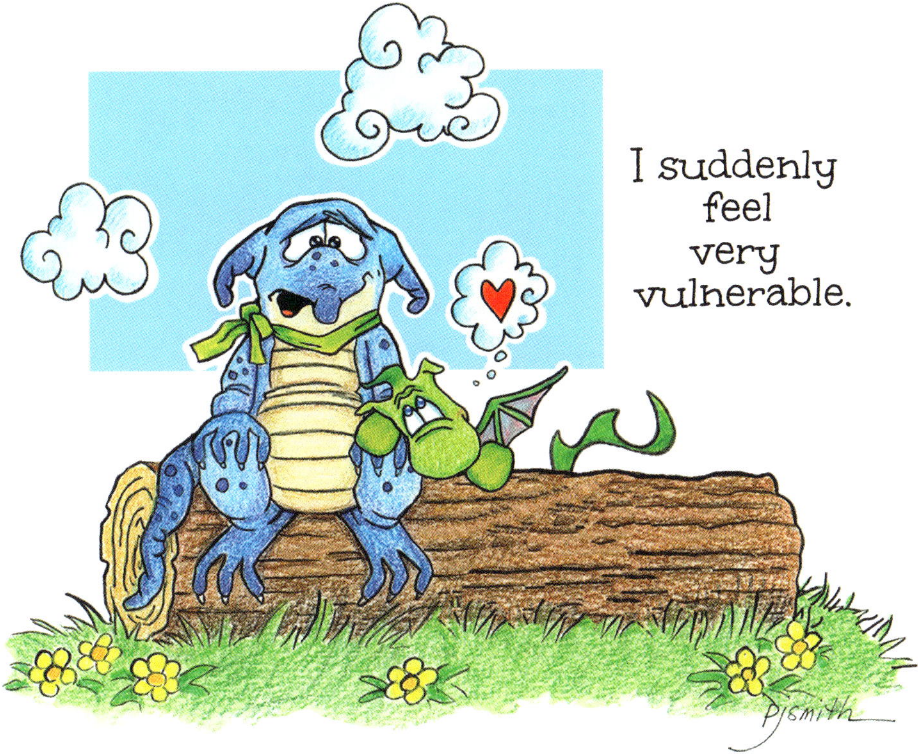

I suddenly
feel
very
vulnerable.

You are
special

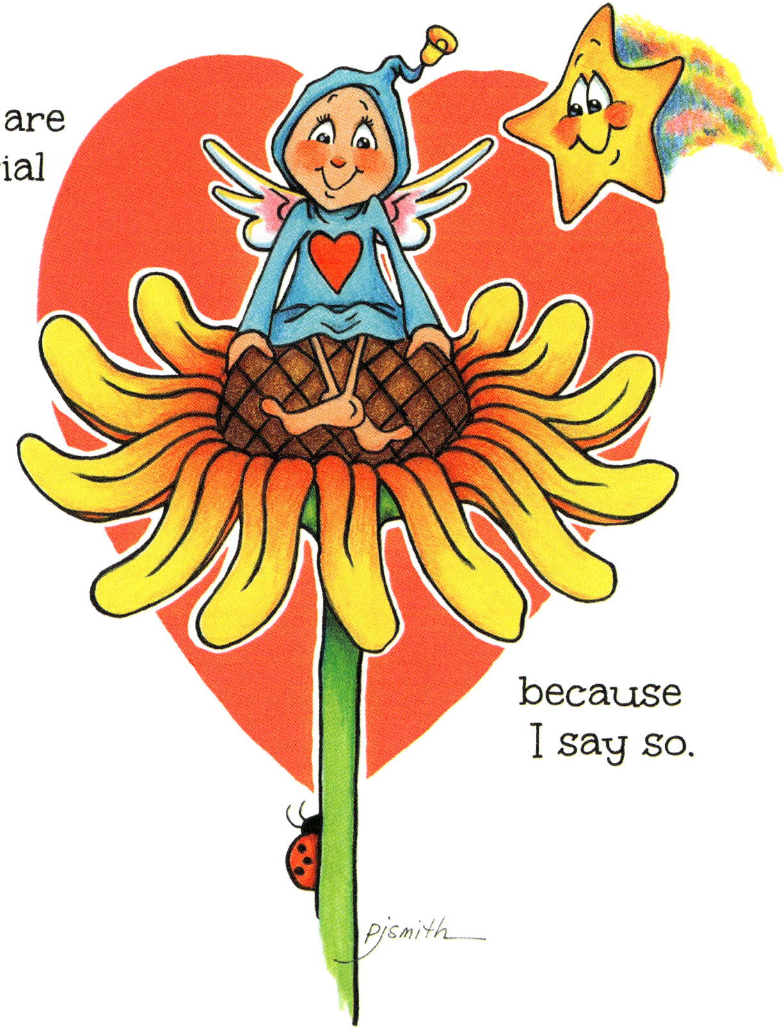

because
I say so.

PJSmith

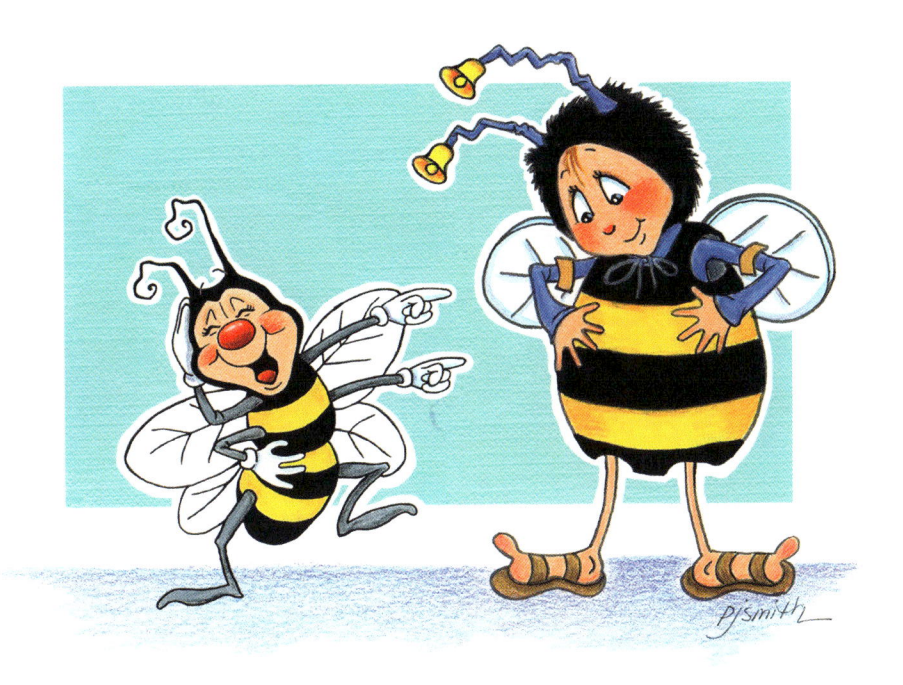

Bee yourself.

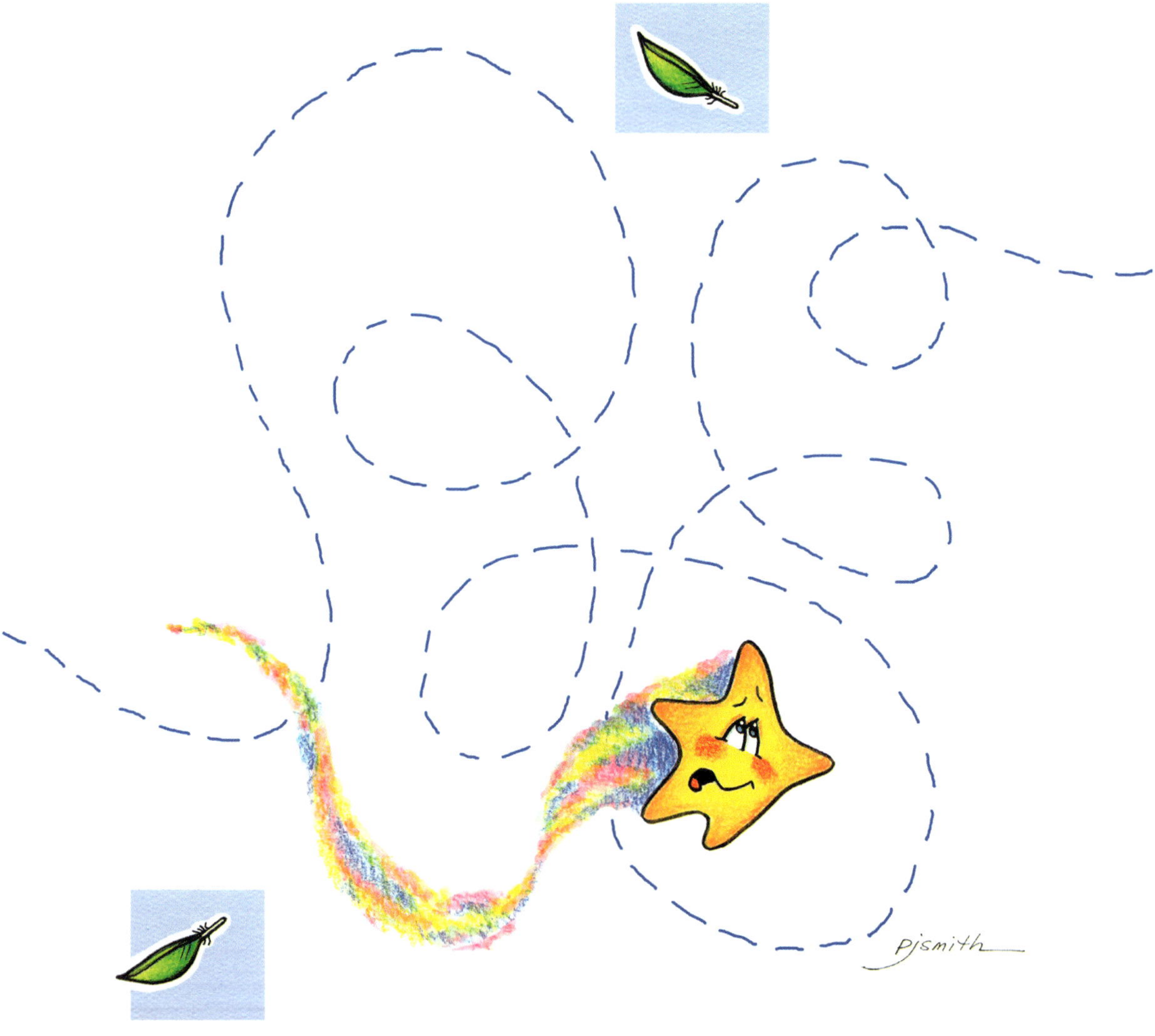
pjsmith

Gratitude
is the
"G force"
to get you moving
in the
best direction.

Just how many Mondays can one week have?

One rainbow

Coming up!

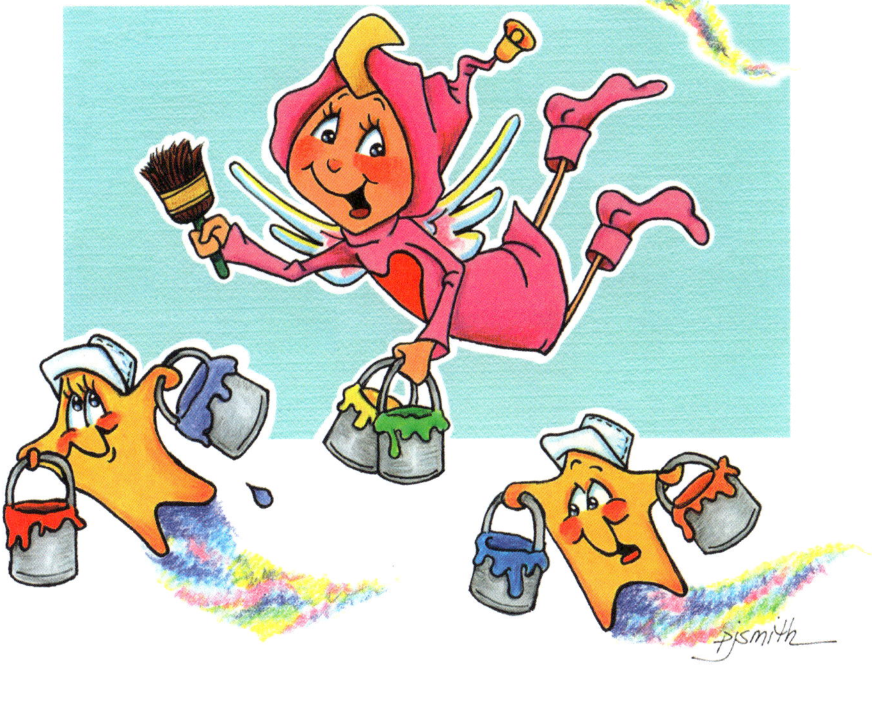

A lovely hat
makes a bad hair day
totally inconspicuous.

And potentially delicious.

How many Imagikins
can fit on the
head of a pin?

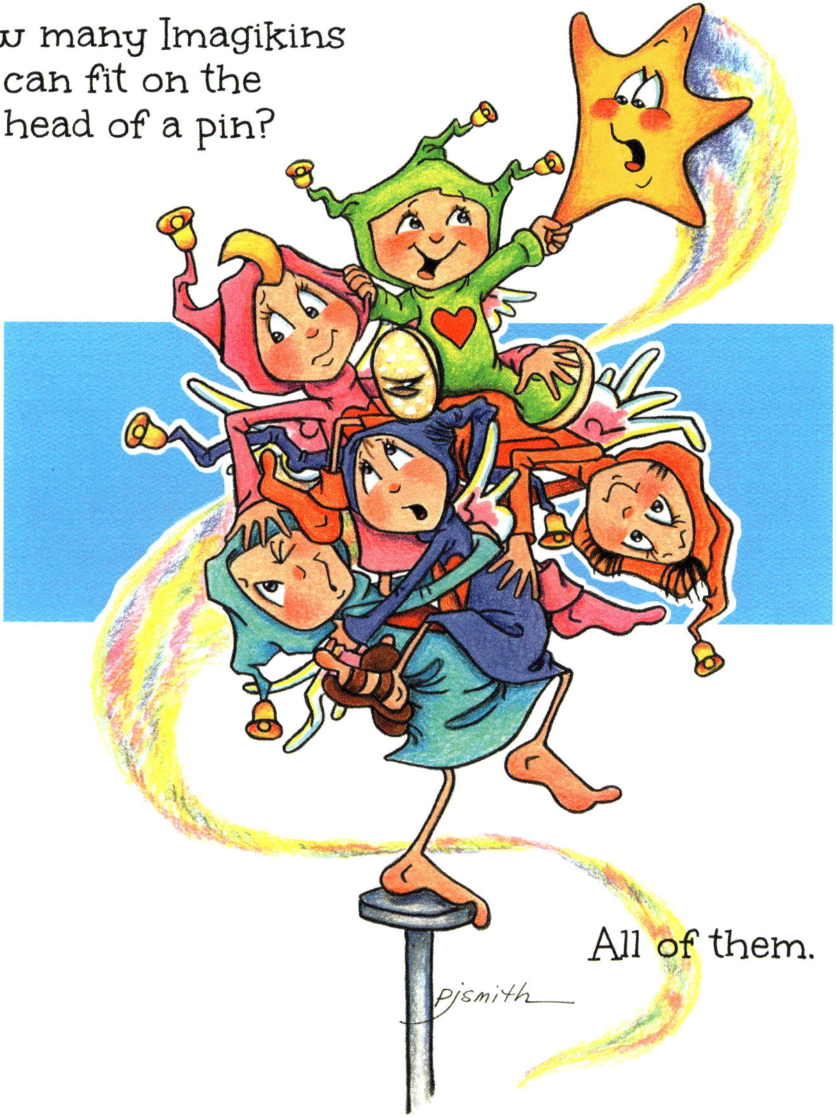
pjsmith

All of them.

One for me . . .
and one for you.

Never let your dragon blow out
your birthday candles.

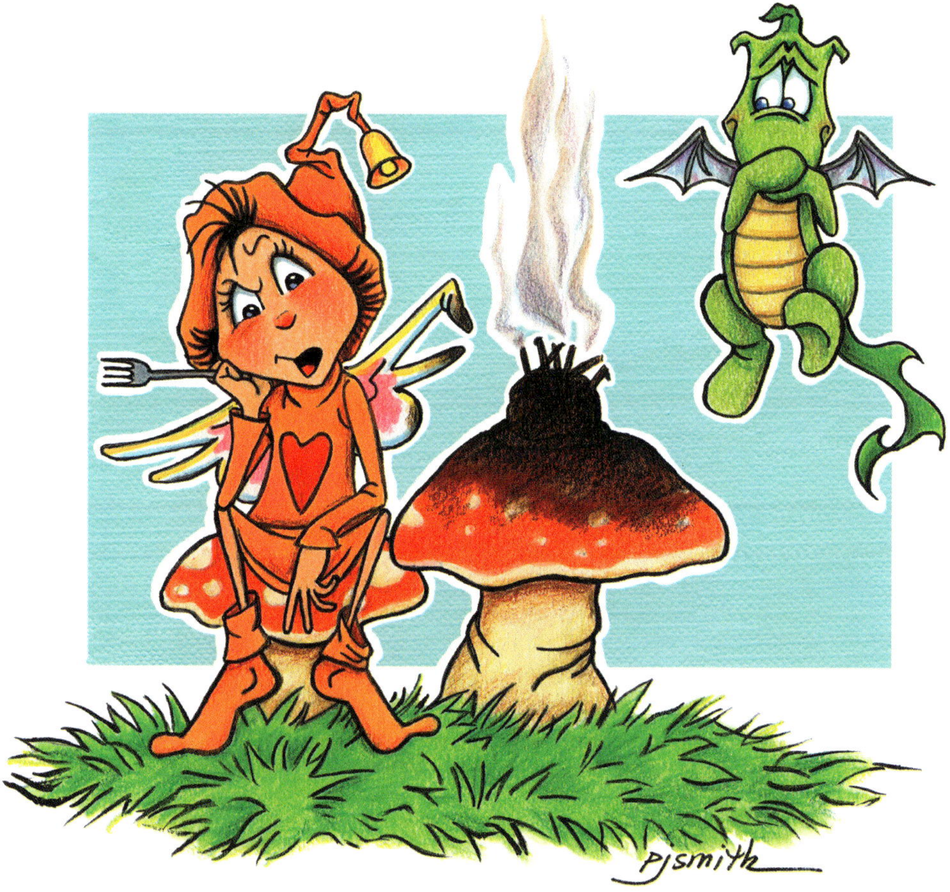
PJsmith

pjsmith

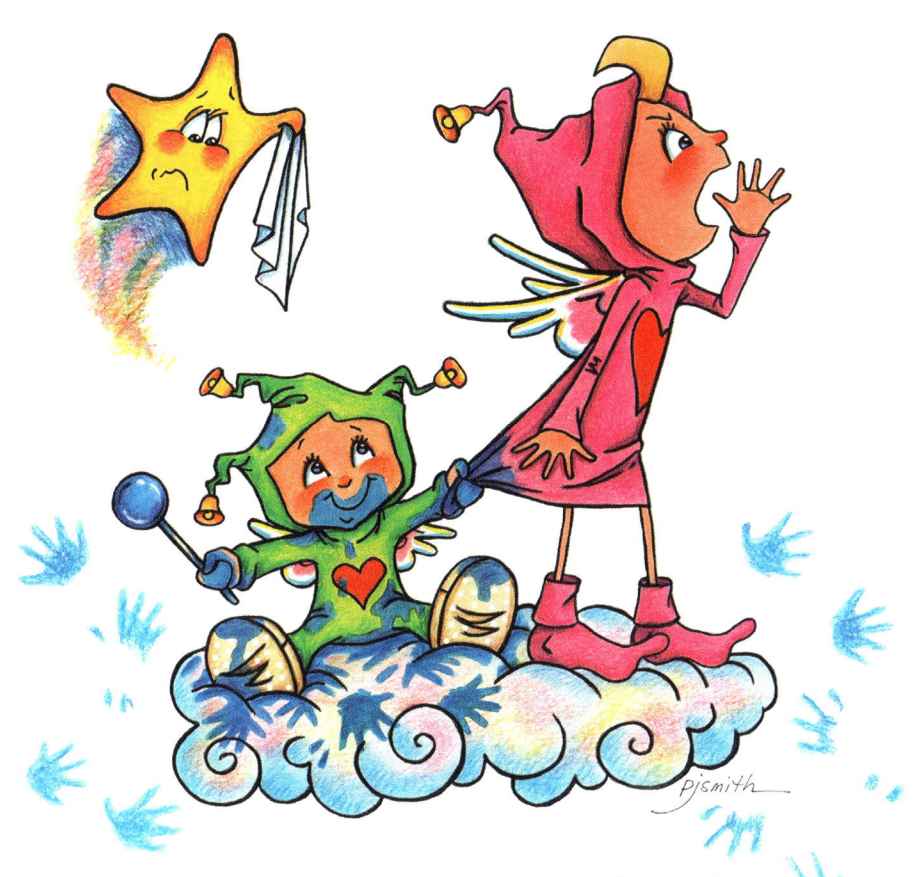

"Clean up on Cloud Nine."

Life
is not
about
waiting
for
the storms
to pass.

It's about
learning
to play
in the rain.

The four most magical words are

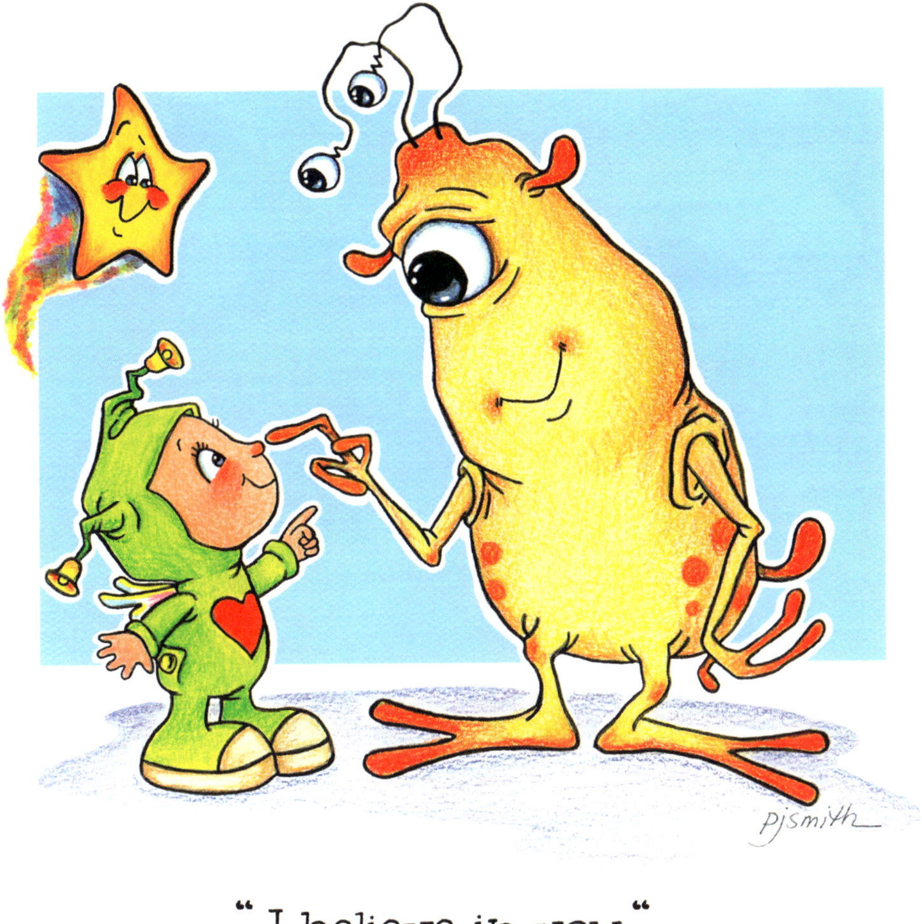
pjsmith

" I believe in you."

Excuse me, God . . .
I need a hug!

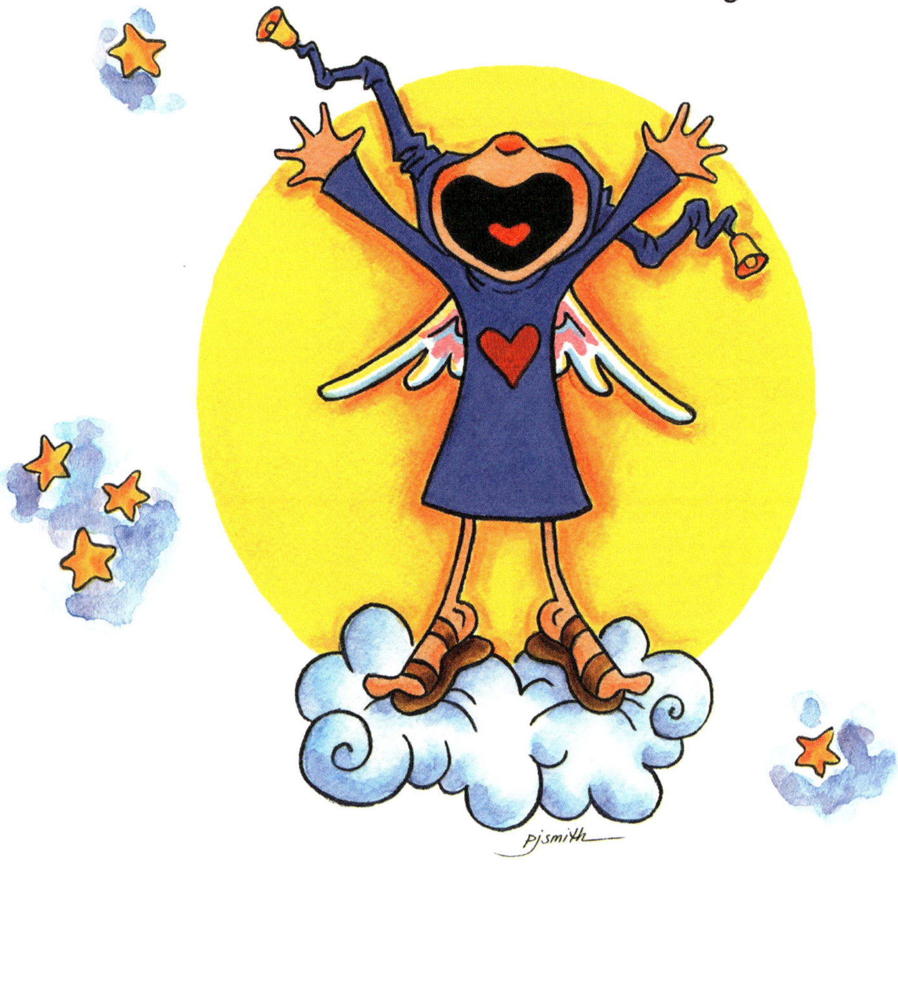

NOW!

A leap of faith is easier with supportive friends,

and a parachute.

Look for the everyday miracles.

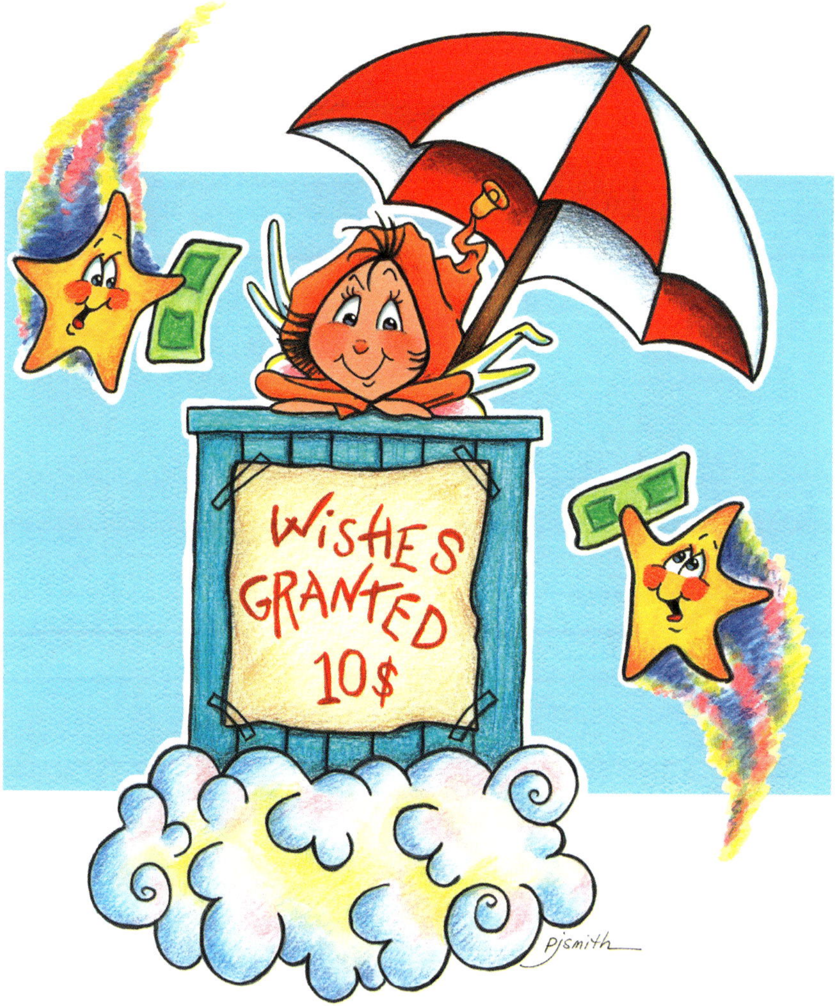
WISHES
GRANTED
10$
pjsmith

Coupon for one wish granted

WISHING GUIDELINES

⭐ Your wish is very important to us.

⭐ Please wait for the next available IMAGIKIN.

⭐ Wishes are answered in the order they are received.
(However... chocolate chip cookies may expedite wish fulfillment.)

⭐ All wishes should be enunciated clearly.
(Note similarities: 'prince charming' vs 'pig farming'.)

⭐ May cause certain side effects such as green skin, eating flies, excessive hopping, etc.
(If side effects do occur, please see your local wizard immediately.)

⭐ IMAGIKINS cannot be held liable for said side effects.

⭐ Due to FDA regulations, magic beans and/or beanstalks are no longer available.

⭐ Wishes for a Fairy Godmother must be directed to the Fairy Godmother's Union at 1-800-GO PMKIN.

⭐ Coupon not valid in the state of California.

TODAY'S FORECAST

Widely splattered showers

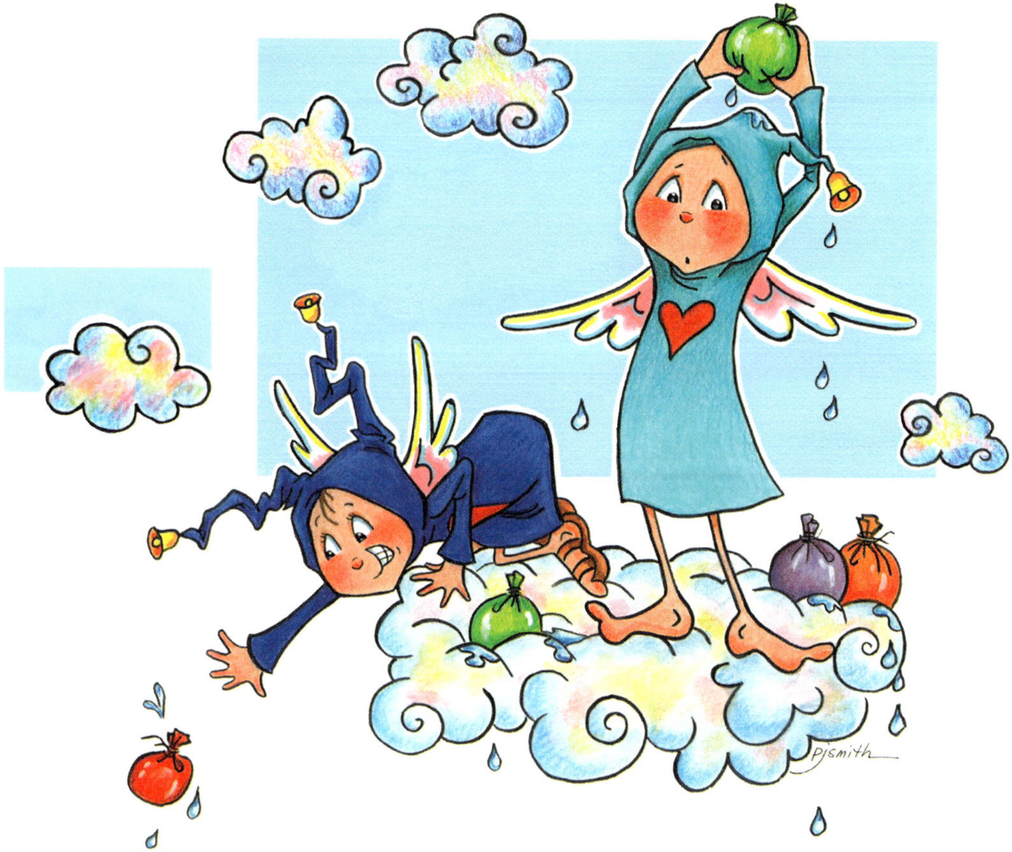
PJsmith

Be somebody's rainbow.

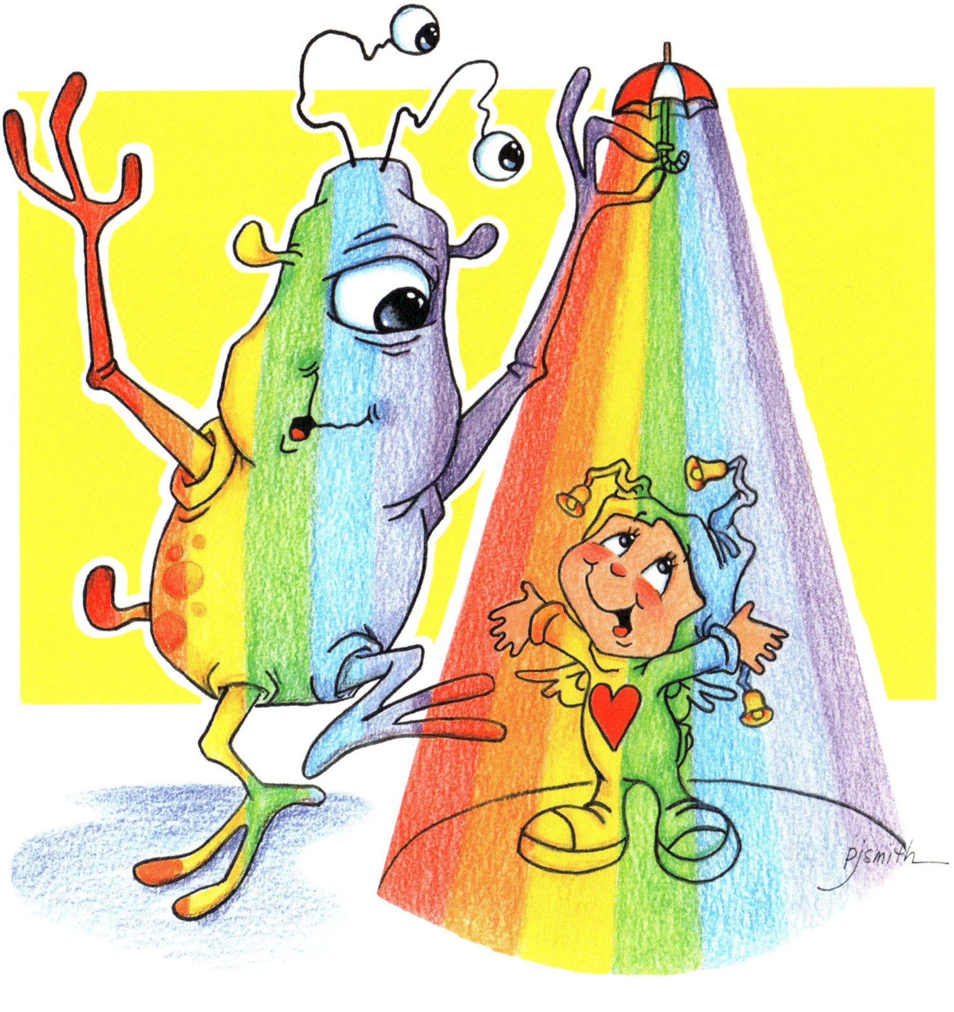
pjsmith

Happiness looks good on you.

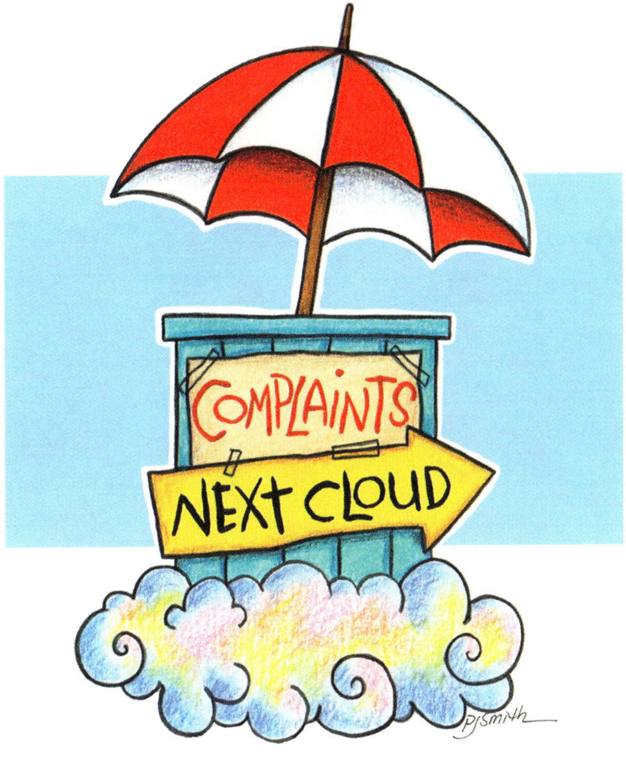
COMPLAINTS
NEXT CLOUD
PJSmith

Love creates the masterpiece.

When you suppose
    you have reached the end,
        it will be just the beginning.

Bandy
Moog
Sparky
Penny
Trevie
Beezu
Peep
Kinden

PJ Smith

Artist, illustrator, author, award-winning
children's furniture designer,
mountain climber, animal lover, part-time angel,
and
Chief Executive Officer of IMAGIKINS affairs.

photo by Stephanie Lynn Hearl

Made in the USA
Columbia, SC
30 October 2017